# Sound-Rage
## A Primer of the Neurobiology and Psychology of a Little Known Anger Disorder

Judith T. Krauthamer

Sound-Rage. A Primer of the Neurobiology and Psychology of a Little Known Anger Disorder is neither a diagnostic tool nor a medical text and is not intended to replace or modify therapy or the diagnostic and medical advice of a licensed practitioner.

A number of the life-experience stories and comments, by individuals who are afflicted with the disorder or by their caregivers, have been taken from online sources. To protect the privacy of all online commenters, the names of all individuals have been changed and all website sources have been aggregated into a single reference.

Published by Chalcedony Press

Copy Edited by: Steven Sokolow
Book Cover Design by Michele A. Danoff, Graphics by Design

ISBN: 978-0-9895035-0-1
Library of Congress Control Number: 2013910331

For correspondences: info@sound-rage.com
2013 website: www.sound-rage.com

# Dedication

The book is dedicated to Dr. May Beresin, a mother who loved her daughters passionately and compassionately. And to all mothers, who know that despite faulty wiring, all children are perfect just the way they are.

# Acknowledgements

This book was written over the course of a year, although it took a lifetime of experience to craft. It was made possible by the help and exceptional talent of a team of experts who contributed to this undertaking.

I am deeply indebted to Katharine Borges, PhD, neuroscientist with the Cold Spring Harbor Laboratory in New York. It would not be hyperbole to say that she vetted each and every neurological reference in the manuscript. She neither accepted nor rejected the book's premises; rather, her commitment was to the absolute accuracy of the science. I am both flattered and grateful for her time and attention. I can't thank her enough.

The therapy section and areas reflecting psychological issues were reviewed by the wise counsel of Noah Weintraub, PsyD, of the Cognitive Behavior Therapy Center of Greater Washington. I'd like to thank him for his advice and mentoring. He is an incredibly compassionate human being. I am humbled by the generosity of his care in his professional practice.

I want to thank my content editor, Laurie Young, CHC, AADP for her thoughtfulness and insight. Her depth of understanding, gleaned from her own extensive experience, added greatly to the manuscript.

I am also indebted to Steve Sokolow, whose copy editing helped to make the research shine. I appreciate the many, many hours he spent attending to details.

I am especially grateful to graphics designer and photographer, Michele Danoff, of Graphics by Design, for creating a beautiful book cover. She encourages and inspires creativity. She is the madam behind Mad Moments photography.

To change the world starts one step at a time and this neurobiology primer is truly a baby step. Dr. Anthony Zador, Program Chair in Neuroscience at the Cold Spring Harbor Laboratory, was immediately encouraging as were Drs. Sukhbinder Kumar and Tim Griffiths of Newcastle University Medical School, and I am grateful that they corresponded so willingly to initial research requests.

I believe that any work that can reduce unnecessary pain and suffering is a worthy undertaking. My dear friend Dr. Hedy Bookin-Wiener, with her vast library and knowledge of all things involving health and wisdom practices, was a wonderful guide. I thank her for sharing the benefit of many years of practice.

Gilda Martinez-Alba, EdD, provided help, encouragement, and support, and wonderful ideas for educating wide audiences. I thank her for opening up new possibilities.

I would like to offer a word of gratitude to Joanne Erde and Susan Hardenbergh for their suggestions for the book cover.

A special note of warmth goes to my family at the Maryland University of Integrated Health (formerly Tai Sophia Institute for the Healing Arts). It was there that I truly learned the value of service and "Give up trying. Practice doing." Susan D., Tracey S., Greg W., Anne B., Tom B., Ann P., Ayo, KoKo, and the entire J12 crowd—I am honored by their presence.

This book would not have been possible without the ongoing love and support of my head cheerleader, David Knipfer. He was my constant reminder of the value of the research. How lucky I am to have such a devoted spouse!

And a final thank you to Wheatie, my furry companion, who slept under my computer desk for nearly a year. Through love we are connected to all living things.

# Contents

# Introduction
## Sound-Rage
### A Primer of the Neurobiology and Psychology
### of a Little Known Anger Disorder

Gum chewing, nose sniffing, pen clicking…For the vast majority of people, these particular sounds are nothing more than background noise. For a small, discrete population these sounds trigger severe and immediate emotional and behavioral responses. Rage and anger swell up immediately; hatred and blame instantly fill the mind. And within seconds the body prepares for flight.

These sounds are just a small sample of the large menu of triggers that can set off a physiological urgency to flee. A widely diverse set of triggers includes more than just sounds. There are visual stimuli that can be equally upsetting, such finger pointing, leg swinging, foot jiggling, and the mere look of someone chewing gum. There are also sensation triggers, such as the repetitive tapping on the back of a person's chair and smelling an unusually strong, unpleasant odor.

In 2001, audiologists[1] coined the collective symptoms as "misophonia," the Greek equivalent of hatred of sounds. Unlike tinnitus (ringing in the ears) and hyperacusis (a health condition characterized by over-sensitivity to certain frequency ranges of sound, or a collapsed tolerance to usual environmental sound),[2] the "hatred of sounds" is not a result of auditory dysfunction. Although used intermittently throughout this primer to describe the syndrome, the term misophonia is a misnomer, since the syndrome encompasses more than just a hatred of sounds. Wikipedia says a misnomer arises because the thing named received its name long before its true nature was known. This appears to be true in the case of misophonia.

Does the sufferer hate the actual sound? Does the sufferer hate whoever or whatever is making the sound? And what about the reaction to finger pointing and other visual stimuli of motion? It makes more sense to identify the syndrome based on its most fundamental characteristic. I believe it is more appropriate to make the connection between anger and the stimuli. There is an immediate anger response to stimuli that are associated with auditory, visual, and olfactory (smell) sensory systems in the brain. Trigger stimuli come from a variety of the senses, yet for the vast majority of people with the disorder the first triggers are sounds. To that end I use the term "Sound-Rage" when referring to the disorder, acknowledging that sounds are the most characteristic trigger for the disorder. However, because the commonly known term is "Misophonia," I will also use that term on occasion.

The terms syndrome and disorder are also used interchangeably. The term disorder requires that two criteria be met: a psychobiological mechanism is malfunctioning, and this underlying dysfunction results in suffering, maladaptation, or both.[See note 1] A syndrome is similarly described as a group of signs and symptoms that together form a pattern or are characteristic of a particular condition.

For purposes of this primer, I have defined "Sound-Rage" as follows:

> *The disorder "Sound-Rage" comprises a unique set of symptoms, most likely attributable to neurological causes unrelated to hearing-system dysfunction. It can be described as an immediate and extreme emotional response of anger accompanied by an automatic physiological flight response and a fundamental discomfort to identifiable auditory, visual, and olfactory stimuli. The disorder disrupts daily living and can have a significant impact on all social interactions.*

In this advanced technological age, why is it that we have never heard about it before? While very little is known about the condition, its recognition is just now being acknowledged in the media. The coined term misophonia is being advanced, however haltingly, in the audiology literature. It can be found in online medical dictionaries[3] but not in the peer-reviewed medical literature. It is included in the 2010 *Textbook of Tinnitus* by its editor, Aage R. Moller, a neuroscientist at the University of Texas at Dallas who specializes in the auditory nervous system.[4, See note 2] The disorder is not yet in the

American Psychiatric Association manual that sets forth diagnostic criteria, descriptions, and other information to guide the classification and diagnosis of conditions.

For the past decade or so, individuals primarily in the United States, England, Netherlands and Australia have sought relief and answers from specialists. In interviews and testimonies, the vast majority of these people state that their practitioners have never heard of the symptoms before. Despite having little, if any, knowledge of the condition, many of the mental health field practitioners, psychiatrists, and psychologists diagnose their patients. These diagnoses are widely diverse and include phobic disorder, obsessive-compulsive disorder (OCD), bipolarity, and manic depressive disorder, as well as anger, control, and behavioral issues.

Due to the community-building capability of the internet, forums have sprung up, encouraging dialogue among sufferers, caregivers, and practitioners. An online yahoo listserve community was established in 2005; this group had grown to roughly 3400 members by 2012. Similar national and international online forums are also on the internet.[5] The collective strength of these groups help to provide a credible voice for the recognition of the condition. Recent media events have also given rise to the acknowledgement of the syndrome as a real, psychological phenomenon.

The disorder might be more prevalent than suspected. On a recent visit with an old friend, I mentioned the research for this book. He countered that he cannot be in the same room as his wife if she is eating an apple. At Christmas dinner, he cannot sit with the family throughout the entire meal because all the eating sounds are too disturbing. Other than those two discrete arenas of discomfort, he does not think at all about having a disorder. In fact, he thought it was just a mild quirk—bothersome only under certain circumstances. An anecdotal study at the Academic Medical Center in Amsterdam states, "The suspicion of a wider spread prevalence of this disorder was supported by the number of patients with misophonia that were (self-) referred to our hospital following an announcement on a Dutch misophonia Internet newsgroup and our hospital website. Within 2.5 years, nearly 50 misophonia patients contacted our hospital."[6]

This primer demystifies the condition. It presents a current state of knowledge to the public and provides another voice for hope, courage, and resilience. I have written it to help those who have struggled for years, in isolation, to see that they are members of a community. Through community there is conversation, resolution, discovery, and connection.

The primer is organized following a sequence for building a broad stroke picture of the disorder. There are three sections, supported by a reference section and note section at the end of the book. In Section I, *Symptoms, Stories, Diagnoses*, I describe the life of a "Sound-Rage" sufferer as she confronts triggers throughout the day. I then present testimonies and stories of people who have the disorder, gleaned from online magazines, interviews, and public online forum biographies, and ordered in such a way as to cohesively describe aspects of the disorder. The quotations taken from these sources are neither re-written nor corrected for spelling. To protect the privacy of all online commenters, the names of all individuals have been changed and all website sources have been aggregated into a single reference. Please refer to note 3 of this introduction regarding the aggregated websites, some of which provided the quotations used in this primer.[See note 3]

I created a non-scientific, short questionnaire for people who think they might have the disorder. The tool for identifying the condition is not a scientifically validated survey but rather an informal assessment. I then present an investigation called "What's the Diagnosis" that evaluates and compares the psychiatric listing of known disorders to the symptoms of "Sound-Rage."

With a basic understanding of what the syndrome looks and feels like, the primer delves into a neurological study of the disorder in Section II, *Neurobiology*. The section presents an overview of how the brain processes information, specifically the triggers. It should be noted here that the disorder is not related to hearing: the disorder is psychiatric, not auditory, in nature. The specific brain parts are examined for their role in the transmission and processing of a trigger starting from when the trigger stimuli first enter the brain.

There is an in-depth look at brain circuitry and multi-sensory processing. This section seeks to explain from a neurological, sensory perspective how triggers expand, from one or two auditory triggers to many auditory, visual, and olfactory triggers.

"Sound-Rage" has all the makings of a developmental disorder. There is a typical age of onset at which there is a change or shift in the way the brain functions. The primer presents a discussion on the few known developmental disorders and possible scenarios of break-downs in the neurology of the brain that result in "Sound-Rage." The book offers the theory that the fundamental change in the brain leads to an auditory trigger assessed by the brain as something other than simply, for example, a chewing sound. The newly dysfunctional brain processes the sound as "danger!" I further postulate a new conceptualization of the neurologic break-down: the brain interprets the sound as "danger!" because neurologically, the sound creates "pain!"

"Sound-Rage" or "Misophonia" disorder differs from all other known disorders in that the automatic response to perceived threat is anger rather than fear. It is well known that anger is a correlate of pain. The primer explores the neurobiology of pain assessment in the brain and demonstrates how the brain can experience the affect or unpleasantness of pain without any actual physical sensation.

The existing literature on anger focuses on "anger and violence" and "anger with aggression," typically in a setting of criminal populations or violent, truant males, and tends to focus on anger leading to destruction and harm. In "Sound-Rage" there is plenty of anger expressed in the form of yelling and crying concurrent to serious thoughts, or cognition, of doing harm. Yet there is very little evidence of a sufferer physically confronting anyone and there is little expression of actual, overt acts of aggression. Raging anger without overt acts of aggression combined with an automatic response for flight behavior is a new paradigm.

The daily onslaught of discomfort generated in "Sound-Rage" is exacerbated by the thoughts and associations that accompany the anger and pain, and this is addressed in Section III, *Emotions, Cognitions, and Therapies.* Through time, the who-what-where pieces of information associated with a trigger and the subsequent pain it causes contribute to the severity and potency of the triggers.

This primer explores and offers possible explanations for why emotionally laden responses exist within the domain of the disorder, especially anger as a function of pain, and how they contribute to the brain's assessment of new sounds, sights, and smells as triggers.

Medical intervention and drugs have not successfully treated the condition because the fundamental, underlying neurological and neurochemical relationships have not yet been established. Although there is no cure, there are a number of therapies and tools that help sufferers cope and live with the syndrome. It is my firm belief that therapies such as cognitive behavior therapy can help the brain re-configure connections and bring relief.

Learning new ways to minimize or calm the automatic response of anger can help alleviate some of the physiological responses of anger. Anger management techniques, pain management techniques, and relaxation practices offer ways for a sufferer to live a fuller, happier life, albeit with "Sound-Rage" lurking in the background. This section carries the critical message that "Sound-Rage" is a neurological disorder that is exacerbated by thoughts and emotions. Sufferers are not doomed to a life-time sentence of unhappiness and they are neither "crazy" nor deficient in any way.

This primer hopes to inspire, intrigue, pique interest, and shift the current conversation by providing research findings and scientific evidence that lead towards the understanding of the disorder. It presents ideas, hypothesizes, and where available, empirical evidence.[See note 4] This primer is not meant to be a definitive scientific treatise; rather, it is a starting point for conceptualizing how the brain processes triggers. Presentation of results from peer-reviewed studies on the brain offer possibility and heuristic value.

---------

What we have is a little known disorder that affects a relatively small population of the world, is virtually unknown in the medical community, and is scarcely recognized by the mental health community. So why am I writing this primer, and why now? For starters, I always believed that one should write what they know. And I know this syndrome well. This insidious and potent disorder is an ongoing visitor in my family. I have first hand and second hand knowledge of the devastating control is has over the sufferer. I know the overwhelming cascade of confusion, sadness, and distance it imposes on close family members. I have been witness to pilgrimages for help from well intended health practitioners that have left the sufferer feeling misunderstood, misdiagnosed, and hopeless.

I was keenly interested in psychology, physiology, and neurology which I studied in college. I became particularly interested in the ways we can shift our thinking about illness when I completed my graduate study at the Maryland University of Integrated Health. If we can look at our points of pain and simultaneously feel personally empowered to deal with them, we can move forward into a happier, healthier life.

I believe that when the community gathers up together and collectively voices the desire to reduce unnecessary pain and suffering, there will be a transformation in the visibility of this yet-to-be documented disorder. I want to be a part of the process that brings relief from pain. As we enter another age of discovery, I want the medical community to specifically and purposefully study this syndrome, to gain an understanding of how the brain can overcome "bad wiring."

The time to create visibility for the disorder is now. Many lives are in turmoil because of the daily barrage of pain caused by the brain misinterpreting innocuous, random sounds and sights. Without the benefit of scientific research, we will be unable to create appropriate medical and pharmacological solutions. Without psychological studies, we will continue to be challenged in creating therapeutic regimes that lead to emotional relief. And without recognition, we will never receive from society-at-large much needed understanding and compassion.

# CHAPTER 1
## A Day in the Life

The coffee pot starts brewing. She gets up from her bed, the one she bought as a spare when she was single. She sleeps on it now, against the wall in the TV room, while an air filtering machine provides white noise. The TV room is at the end of the hall. Its door remains closed; the window remains closed. Outside, the neighbors' dogs barking can barely be heard. The snoring down the hall is audible only after the air filter is turned off and the door is opened.

Another morning and she still rises alone, despite being married. She wonders if her children think this is odd, parents who get on quite well but who have separate sleeping quarters. She has long since stopped worrying about its impact on intimacy. She has got to get sleep and her husband's breathing entraps her in a state of unmitigated tension. She cannot get comfortable if there is even a hint of snoring. Any guttural sound is like electricity going through her. She has tried ear plugs but they have hurt her ears. And even when they block out the sound she finds she is actually listening for it: the first hiss of a snore. There is just as much tension in waiting for the noise as there is in actually hearing it. She knows her husband feels the distance and is lonely. She knows that her inability to be at ease in his soft breathing is damaging to the marriage. But she can't do it. She cannot lie next to the breathing sounds. It just isn't worth the misery.

She drinks her coffee and eats quickly. In just a few minutes the family will begin tottering down the stairs to the kitchen. Out will come the milk, the bowls, the spoons and the cereal. Her heart starts to speed up; she is behind schedule, and in one minute the clinking of silverware will send her running from the kitchen. Just the thought of the family—especially her husband—chomping on crunchy frosted flakes and slurping hot coffee begins a slow dance of anxiety. She throws the coffee cup into the sink, barely aware of its close call with calamity as it smashes against the stainless steel. Her husband is now in the kitchen. She forces a huge smile and greets him.

Internally, she is beginning to panic. She cannot stand next to him as he pours a cup o f Maxwell House. The anticipation of that first slow deliberate sip pushes her even further. She has got to get away, now!

In the early morning rush hour traffic, she pulls into the commuter bus parking lot extra early. It is a pre-emptive move; she can pick which bus seat to claim. It is always a crap shoot. She can try to navigate to where she thinks the quiet people will sit, but there is always an element of randomness. She sits next to the window, looking out, feeling more and more nervous as the various commuters get on the bus. Turning her head, she smiles coyly at the very quiet young man but there is no connection. He walks on. She thinks to herself, "If those kids who work at the hospital sit behind me, I will kill myself." The two of them talk, non-stop. One of them has sibilance; he whistles as much as he talks. The high pitched noise is a death knell. Just the thought of them talking stirs hatred— actual, real, visceral rage.

Fortunately, the older man who reads the paper cover to cover has walked several rows back. The consistent sound of the newspaper rustling is a major disturbance. "Stop folding the damn paper already" she says to herself whenever he is within earshot. A large, middle aged woman sits down next to her. "Oh God," she moans to herself, "this has got be my karma." Her seat mate is chewing gum. She can feel the tears begin to well in her eyes as she pulls out her full-ear coverage Bose headphones. It will be forty five minutes of focusing on loud music, to the exclusion of all else.

Bus ride over, she briskly walks to her office, into the cubicled human resources department. Here, professional workers are paid well to sit three feet from one another with nothing more than a six foot tall padded barrier between them. Phone conversations and chatter are a matter of course. The more white noise, the better. She has already moved her desk in the small square footage allotment to be as far away as possible from neighbors' computers. The click-click-click sound of fingernails on the keyboard put her in a state of pent up anxiety.

Today it is the subtle, insidious iPod noise coming from her colleague's cheap ear buds that makes her wary. It is a daily challenge, one that has an impact on her productivity. It will be impossible to focus on the day's tasks with the intrusion of that noise. With each squeak from the iPod she feels her personal space invaded. It is as if the energy from the sound is a personal attack. She can wear her Bose headphones while she works on documents but she will have to take them off eventually so that she can respond to the phone calls. It is not quite nine in the morning and her body is positioned for defense.

Her day goes, as do all other days, with the general risks and rewards of making a living. It is a good day if she does not have to cope with someone cracking their gum. It is an especially good day if no one in the office has a cold. On those days, the constant, rhythmic sniffing coming from an undisclosed cubicle is torture. For each sniff she thinks to herself, "Shut the hell up! What kind of idiot are you coming to work when you're sick? It's disgusting." She can feel the animosity build. The need to know exactly who is sniffing is overwhelming, and she will walk around the floor, zeroing in on the sound. Once she knows who has the cold she will focus her anger and hatred on them. She will get some work done but the important work requiring concentration will be deferred to another day.

The bus ride home is a repeat of the morning. Her first thought is to look out over the seated people to decipher who is not chewing gum. There is also the chance that someone might be sporting a horrible body odor that will fill her nostrils and her personal space. Her body prepares for the flight feelings that she knows all too well. She will remain guarded until the bus has completed all of its pick up stops and heads out of the city.

After she is home for a while, and having completed all the daily living chores of picking up kids' clothing, feeding the dog, and checking the mail, she begins dinner. It is a chore she does lovingly, knowing that it nourishes her family. The children and their father sit at the table. She puts the plates of food in front of them and hurriedly leaves the room. The dining ritual is one in which she will not participate. With her plate, she makes her way upstairs to the TV room. As she climbs the stairs she is happy to hear talking, laughter, the sharing of worlds. Until the silverware clicks against the dishes.

Then the door once again closes, and she can be in a quieter place. There is no choice—the isolation from the noise is absolutely necessary.

The evening is filled with homework, conversations, a family walking in and out of one another's radar screens. There are small, intermittent internal battles. Her husband, in talking about his day, uses too many words that begin with "p" and "k." Each word produces a tiny jolt of pain. Within an instant some part of her heart hardens and her loving husband repulses her. She cannot stand to look at his lips. She repeats back the "puh" "puh" sounds as if making those sounds will calm her. Her husband takes note and stops talking. She simultaneously feels sorrow and grateful for the silence.

It is time for bed. After the children are settled in for the night she tenderly kisses her husband on the cheek. "Good night. I'm going to bed," she says. Her husband faces her. "It's freezing in the bedroom," he says, filled with longing, loneliness, the desire to connect. "Turn on the electric blanket," she replies, and doggedly turns away, heading for the quiet of the TV room.

Before she goes to sleep, she runs through her day, in fast forward. Long-winded conversations are boiled down to a sentence. She ponders a dilemma at work; she worries about her daughter's upcoming project. She reminds herself to buy her tickets for her upcoming travel abroad. As she settles into sleep she sorts her experiences so as to keep moving forward. But she does not consider, not even for a moment, how she spent her day fending off assault. She does not consider the physical hardship of protecting herself, over and over. She does not think about the impact of short intense bursts of rage and the emotional intensity of hatred. It is as if she has accepted that she lives a divided life: one that is normal and one that requires ongoing escape routes. It is as if the constant vigilance for sounds and shaking legs and smells, to the exclusion of a world of thoughts, has become her mental landscape.

# CHAPTER 2
## Stories and Testimonies from the Community

*Conscious states exist only from a first-person point
of view. They are ontologically subjective, meaning
they only exist when experienced by a conscious
agent and cannot be redefined independently of the
experiencer. Consequently, they cannot be eliminated
in favor of third-person references to instrument-
based measures of behavior, physiological activation,
or neural events. It is not possible to measure more
easily observable aspects of emotion (e.g., facial
movements, vocal acoustics, voluntary behaviors,
peripheral physiology) to learn something about its
subjective aspect. To know what emotion feels like, it
is necessary to ask people what they experience.[1]*

You are reading this primer because the title piqued your interest, or
perhaps someone you know has asked you repeatedly (in words that
were polite, not so polite, filled with indignation, or downright
derogatory) to stop chewing your gum so loudly. Maybe you find
yourself getting very upset when you hear the bass notes coming
from your neighbors' stereo, to the point where you have to find the
quietest place in your house to cover your ears. Someone whom you
love very much cannot stand to sleep beside you or eat a meal with
you, and you simply cannot understand why. Perhaps your child,
who is usually filled with wonder, happiness, and "normalcy," has
started putting her hands over her ears whenever you sniff, and cries
out when you wash the dishes by hand.

Life-experience stories, as told by the people who are afflicted with
the disorder or by the people who live with them, offer great
insights. I present stories from interviews, public website forums,
and the comment sections from the online sites of television
programs, newspapers, and magazines.[2]

Stories are also used throughout this primer to give voice to the
experience of those who are afflicted, to annotate specific ideas, and
to challenge pre-conceived ideas about how the brain works. Many

of these stories have been abridged, but none have been edited or spell-corrected. (The names of all individuals have been changed to protect privacy and all sources have been aggregated to further insure privacy.)

I present a biography or story that reveals the life experiences of a sufferer, taken from an interview I conducted in which I asked general questions such as, *When did you first notice your symptoms? Have they evolved, grown or lessened?* and *What challenges do you face?* I then present a series of short stories or testimonies. The first set of testimonies describes the age of onset of symptoms and how those symptoms manifest in the person's life. The second set refers to the changes of symptoms through time: how symptoms, triggers, and reactions change. The third set describes how people live with anger and other facets of general triggers. The fourth set presents stories about visual triggers. The final set looks at the familial aspects of the disorder.

You will note that through each story the speaker describes feelings, thoughts, and associations. There is an authenticity to how each person describes his/her life experience. You most likely will see trends and similarities. It is through these similarities that the syndrome can be more clearly defined and ultimately researched.

Stories that reveal life experiences

Interview with Nikki:  I vaguely remember the onset.  I was in elementary school, around seven or eight years old. My father was eating and out of nowhere the sound coming from his mouth was just unbearable. I don't remember any details about how our family interacted in general. It was only a short matter of time before the eating issue became prevalent in my life and dictated the family dynamic of tension, yelling and fighting. It goes without saying that a family with a child having hysterics at dinner time becomes dysfunctional rapidly. Maybe our family was already a dysfunctional one and it became increasingly frenetic and out of control. I believe that no one really understood what was going on but I do think that it caused my mother a great deal of angst and worry.

Noises from eating were definitely the first thing that caused a reaction. From there other sounds became just as unbearable. My sister took piano lessons and would clip her fingernails. Each nail (clip) would send me into a rage. I would scream "Stop it!" from my room. My mother washing dishes was excruciating. (Stop clicking the dishes!") There were other sounds that didn't actually result in an immediate reaction of rage and hatred but made me very internally nervous and tense. The continuous humming of my next door neighbor's air conditioner comes to mind. The tension and anxiety would slowly build up until my internal barometer for exploding was too great. In all cases I would run to any room to get away from the sound.

I also was deeply perturbed by motion. My sister had a habit of twirling her hair. She would take her thumb and forefinger and lift a few strands of hair. It was a nervous habit but to me it felt like the energy of her twirling her hair was torturous. In school I would become very anxious and nervous if someone sat cross legged and swung their legs.

School became a daily ritual of unhappiness. In my middle and high school we had study periods where people just sat at their desks. There was no talking. There would only be the sound of people cracking gum from all corners of the room. I would sit in total agony, but my mind would race with thoughts of incredible hatred. It is impossible for anyone who does not have this disorder to fully understand the impact and power of that hatred. You wish the person dead! It is as if nothing else exists but to get that sound to stop. Once the chewing sound is gone my mind relaxes and my body starts to relax.

The intensity of the reactions has never diminished. The range of things that disturbs me has not diminished. As I get older new sounds and visuals or motions disturb me. I have arranged my life to accommodate living with the things that upset me. I cannot have an apartment near tennis or basketball courts: I can't abide the bouncing balls. I have to have sound proofed walls or carpets: I get very anxious if there are any undertones from a TV or stereo coming from next door. Conversations from another apartment are also very disturbing. A neighbor's barking dog can drive me to distraction. Work has presented a number of challenges. Not having a private office is difficult: I cannot focus or concentrate if I can hear sounds from other peoples' headphones. On occasion, the sound of typing on a keyboard is disturbing. The subway can be an exercise in anger, particularly if the entire commute is next to someone chewing or listening to music through inexpensive earbuds. As much as I love to fly, if someone is talking non-stop or has an over sibilant "s" from several rows away I become excessively nervous.

I have to say that the inability to live with certain noises and sights has not stopped me from living a full and mostly happy life, but it has limited certain activities. I do not go to movies as often as I would like because of people chewing popcorn. I cannot go to the theater without anxiety. Inevitably, someone in the audience will be sniffing. It takes me a while to settle in, to make sure that the people around me will not set off a reaction. I adore my husband, but his pointing at things is very disturbing. When we travel he cannot point to places on the map. He picks up a stick or a pencil and uses it as a pointer.

I have asked my sister if she has any symptoms or reactions to sounds. She claims that people chewing gum makes her nervous although it has never stopped her from attending any public event or venue. She believes her noise aversion is much milder than mine. Like me, my sister is in good health. Neither of us has a "diagnosed" psychological problem and neither has ever had a serious illness or disease. We are both non-smokers. I guess the only other physical or psychological issue I have is that I have a habit of picking at my skin.

I have tried anti-depressants but they have had absolutely no impact on the symptoms or their severity. I take mega doses of supplements and meditate on a near daily basis. Good nutrition, exercise, adequate sleep and meditation have all helped me to be productive and to live a fulfilled life, but again, have had no effect on my symptoms. I have tried psychotherapy and did not find it useful or practical. I use earplugs and expensive headphones for travel and a white noise machine to block out noises at home and at work.

Throughout my life, people close to me and strangers elicit the same responses, hatred, rage, nervousness, anxiety. Although I have noticed one interesting thing: if a sound is bothering me and I identify its origin, sometimes all physiological and psychological responses go immediately back to normal. Here is an example. If I am on a commuter train and I hear a clicking sound that I think is someone popping gum, I become immediately agitated. But if I notice that the clicking sound is from something else, like the window rattling, then I return to a non-agitated state.

There is one exception to everything. When I had children, I made the mental decision to not allow any of their eating noises or habits to have an impact on me. To this day, my children are the only people whose eating sounds have no effect on me. Interestingly, this has given me a unique perspective on my problem.

When I think of people eating my brain automatically thinks negative and hateful thoughts.But when I eat breakfast with my children and they are crunching away on cereal, the sounds simply do not register. They are no more unique or disturbing than the washing machine running or birds chirping or the school bus up the street. It makes me absolutely aware that the noises that diminish me completely are normal. Eating is normal, breathing is normal. Sniffing, hacking and throat clearing are all normal human activity. The disorder I have has so reconfigured my brain that it hardly has the capacity for recognizing that sound is neither good nor bad. It simply is.

Stories about age of onset

Based on the testimonies, there is a range of ages for onset, with some testimonies recognizing an onset as early as four and others as late as the early twenties. Both the United States Centers for Disease Control and Prevention (CDC) and the World Health Organization (WHO) define the age range for adolescents as 10-19. The stories indicate an age of onset in childhood—ages five to ten—and at or just prior to puberty (early adolescence)—roughly ages 11 through 13.

Sueanne's Story:  I seem to remember starting to notice I had an issue with eating noises when I was about 9 or 10 years old. I found myself unable to stand being in the same room with my dad when he was eating, sucking or chewing something. I had to block out the sound and it made me want to cry. Every smack of his lips felt like a jolt of electric anger through me.

Stephanie's story: I have had this problem for most of my life. It started suddenly when I was 8 or 9 years old. It hasn't stopped since then. I hate the sound of the letter P in spoken words. It's the little bit of saliva that escapes from a person's lips when they say words like: Pine, Alpine, Pile, Pie, Pint... It just sounds so spitty, so wet, and that's what I hate. I am also bothered by the sound of the letters C, K and G. The "cuh" sound in words like Cake, Walk, Car, Cat, Cop... and so on. I can't do anything with my life because of it.

Darin's story: Around 6 years old, my Mom's snapping of her gum began to bother me. She was a prolific gum chewer and almost every other chew of her jaw would produce a pop from her gum. Soon it was not just the snapping that bothered me but merely the sight of her chewing gum [actual popping noise still produced the most rage]. When exposed to someone else who was popping their gum, I would flee if I could.

Erik's Story: I first remember being bothered by chewing sounds and the sight of my mother eating or chewing gum, the way she moved her jaw when eating, as well as the sound of my stepfather slurping drinks and soup, when I was around 13 or 14 years old.

Lorin's Story: I've been this way since about 1st grade and then it got worse in middle school/high school. In second grade we had to write an essay about how we would change the classroom if we could. I wrote about an elaborate setup where we were each in our own little soundproof booths and all our papers were put through little tubes to us. It was my dream!

Andrea's Story: I have had "oversensitive ears" since I was at least 5 years old, I am now 38 and the annoying mouth sounds, gum chewing, food crunching, breathing, sniffling, throat clearing, nail biting, snoring, and on and on, are getting worse by the day. I am also bothered by snack bags crumpling and anticipate every move my trigger people make, even on the phone! I am on the verge of either quitting my job or losing my job, my family and my sanity. My first question to those I love, generally is what are you eating or are you chewing gum? which is the thing I despise the most and will shoot dirty looks, retreat, lash out angrily or run away. I am at my wits end.

Carlos's Story: Since I was around seven or eight I have had an absolute abhorrence of lip smacking and loud chewing. Twenty-some years later and I still can be put IMMEDIATELY into a foul, sometimes downright angry, mood on hearing someone noisily chewing and popping gum. Thoughts of ripping the offending chewing gum out of the person's mouth or asking them what the heck is wrong with them that they have to make those noises. Nice to know I'm not just randomly pissed off by people lacking in manners....but, seriously, why DO people feel the need to make such noises in the first place?

Tanya's story: I have suffered from this since the age of 7 or 8. There is never a day I don't encounter a trigger noise of some sort. Typing and eating sounds are the worst for me. I work in a cubicle environment, and must wear headphones 8 hours a day. This often causes me to get tension headaches, from the headphones pressing on my temple and ear area, but there is no way I can go without them. I have seen several family doctors, psychiatrists and psychologists, with no help. I have taken several different anti-depression medications and anti-anxiety medications. I have found nothing to help.

Stories about triggers increasing through time

Dick's Story: Soon, my family's breathing noises began to bother me. Sleeping with someone else in the room was terrible. I couldn't stand hearing the clink and clatter of my family using their spoons/knife/forks while eating. My Dad would sit with his legs crossed and the ankle of his crossed leg he would rotate around and around and around. I couldn't stand this. Up through high school, the number of items that bothered me "grew" slowly.

And here's an interesting observation: the original, primary irritation of my Mom's popping gum that enraged me so much, if a stranger popped their gum, it would produce a huge reaction from me while if this stranger did something that was a "secondary" irritation, it wouldn't bother me as much. As I got older this began to change. I was noticing I could no longer go to a movie because of all the people eating their ****ing popcorn. All that chewing noise would just enrage me. Now it wasn't just my family's chewing noises but others chewing crunchy stuff that would do it. Into college and for the last 20 years since, my irritations have grown to include many more things and my reactions to them are stronger and quicker. I can't even stand to have the TV on a baseball game because so many of the players chew gum. Clicking, snapping noises are bad, finger nail clippers are the worst.

SueAnne's story: I'm still unable to deal with my dad's eating noises and I seem to be growing more sensitive to other noises as well, such as clicking pens, noisy pipes, rustling sweet and crisp wrappers. Also, a big one for me is hearing other people's music through their headphones or mobile phones when on public transport.

William's Story: I think my 14 year old daughter may have misophonia. I stayed up for hours last night searching the internet (yet again) trying to figure out what is going on with her. For at least 9-10 months now, things have been bothering her, and it's getting worse. It started out with her not being able to tolerate ANY noise (except the TV) or movement while she was doing homework (hard to accomplish in a house with four teenage girls). A couple months into all this, she became totally intollerant (sp) of anyone coughing (and often just clearing their throat), and she either makes a "humming noise" or screams "freak!" when someone coughs. Now she cannot stand to eat with two of her sisters.

It seems there are more and more triggers, and her responses come across as totally irrational. The rage on her face is terrifying, and her sisters said she is starting to respond (with the humming) when around friends (I don't know about school), whereas until recently it was only with immediate family members. It does not bother her if she coughs, only others. She is also a perfectionist, and in all the research I've done, I've wondered if part of her problem isn't OCD, but nothing really, totally fit.

Victoria's Story: Initially it was only the chewing sounds of people I knew well that bothered me. Now everybody bugs me. As is the case with most of those who've posted, I am not only bothered by chewing sounds but a multitude of other sounds as well -- the list seems to be growing. I cannot stand the sound of a spoon hitting a dish, typing, my dog licking herself (I suppose that fits under the chewing category - YUK!), breathing, sniffling, most types of fidgeting sounds, and simply watching people eat with their mouths open even if I cannot hear them. Within the past year, I have come to be equally disturbed by others' movements -- the action of moving their arm to eat (i.e. a bucket of popcorn), working a crossword puzzle, shaking a leg, sliding their fingers on a wet glass or bottle. If the movement is consistent or predictable, it's really annoying.

My poor husband (of 24 years) has had about all he can take with it and the stress it has been put on him trying his best to avoid upsetting me. Our marriage is at risk now. The list of sounds and motions that bother me is growing. I've been in therapy for years. Seventeen years ago, I went back to therapy (after about five years in therapy dealing with issues of having been sexually abused). My therapist thought the anger I developed in response to chewing sounds was related to unsolved anger towards my step-father (the abuser). That sounded like a logical cause for me. Still, many years later I've successfully dealt with issues related to sexual abuse but continue to face feelings of rage associated with sounds. My response to the sounds/movements are anger, rage, as well as a desire to physically hurt the offender. My heart starts beating faster, my hands start shaking, and I feel like I'm going to explode!

Maureen's Story: My 8 year old daughter has always had "sensitive ears"...loud noises have always bothered her. About a year and a half ago she started verbalizing her irritability with people who "smack". While "smacking" is an annoying behavior that I do not allow in our home, her response became even more unbearable. It went from hearing smacking noises of other eating to hearing snacking noises while others are simply speaking or breathing. I initially thought she was acting out and being respectful, but have realized that she is truly struggling. Her sound sensitivity has progressively gotten worse. As school she covers her ears when those who "smack" or "make the s or t sound" and is clearly distracted. At home, she lets all of that frustration out. The mere sound of my voice (which is hardly a high pitched or overly soft voice) causes her to cover her ears, hit them, often scream out. We cannot have dinner as a family, I cannot help her with her homework, I cannot be mom. It is absolutely heartbreaking!

We went to an ENT Specialist yesterday. He had her hearing tested and she did show signs of sensitivity to sounds within a certain frequency that typically does not bother others. Unfortunately, I was told that there isn't much they can do and she will likely grow out of it. The ENT Specialist did say he was going to contact a colleague who is a professor, Otolaryngology, Neurotology, and Pediatric Otolaryngology and see if he had any suggestions. I should hear something in a week. I just feel hopeless right now. I need to be able to be "mom" and my daughters hearing issue is preventing that. More than anything, I hurt for her...she must feel so isolated and misunderstood.

## Stories of anger: living with triggers

Jerry's story: It gets so horrible. I will be in my room and just hear the noise of silverware clinking against a plate and get really angry. I find it hard to concentrate at the movie theater, too. If someone is slurping or chewing or crinkling their wrapper, I won't be able to concentrate on the movie. It will ruin the whole experience. . If someone lifts their water bottle, I have to block my ear and turn because I know they will make a gulping noise. If I'm stuck near someone chewing loudly, I have to block them from view and hold my ear so I don't see or hear them. And if I hear gulping or chewing or loud breathing directly, I get this feeling like I need to rub my ear afterwards.

Lyndon's Story: What I dont understand is how it could NOT be annoying to be around the gum popping and chomping. How do these chomping smacking popping people not drive themselves insane? How do their jaws not ache from the constant chewing? I too get ANGRY when I hear the gum cracking, etc. I cannot concentrate on anything else when I hear it. I am the same way with sniffing. Disgusting. And people are so oblivious of how disgusting they are. I have gotten pretty balls-y over the years, asking people to stop chomping their gum. I have a close friend that chews gum constantly and I find myself saying no to hanging out with her when I feel like I just cant take it that day. My dad has the constant sniffing problem and it has DEFINITELY affected our relationship. It is literally 24 hours a day sniffing. Sometimes I count the seconds between sniffs...I rarely get to 5. I cant even stand to be in the same room with him.

Sometimes I can tolerate eating with people because I tell myself it will be over soon, they wont eat forever - but gum chewing can last HOURS. I was on a small road trip with my friend the other day - she ate about 25 doritos and then IMMEDIATELY put a piece of gum in her mouth. Not enjoyable. She laughs, tells me to relax, etc. My mother said to me my whole life that if it were up to me I would ask people to stop breathing. People do not understand how this feels - it is not something you can just 'relax' away. It makes me want to rip my skin off...and then theirs. I find it amazing how many people are constantly chewing...I make and receive many many phone calls a day at my job and I would say HALF the people I talk to have something going on in their mouth. Disgusting. I know someone who is like me and said she went on Paxil and it helped. I really dont want to medicate myself but at age 34, I can tell it is getting worse, not better.

Brittany's Story: I have to suppress the urge to fly into a socially unacceptable rage on an almost daily basis thanks to this. The cat licking his butt in the middle of the night, anybody chewing their food, that squeaky sound my bike is making, that crazy lady chewing gum and yapping on the phone in the waiting room. UGH.

Allison's story: I can't stand the smacking of lips while one is eating or talking, the unnecessary rattling of the paper or wrapper off a piece of candy, popping of gum, snoring, the dog chewing on his beloved bone, someone tapping a quarter on the counter repetitively, the absentminded clicking of a pen while working or talking, the repetitive sighs someone does cause they are bored in front of me...or across the room, or down the hall...I can hear it all. Over dinner in a crowded restaurant, my company is intently listening to me talk and I try to "stay with" the conversation, all the while I hear the clanking of dishes and scrapes of forks and knives and plates throughout the restaurant, the crying baby across the room, the toddler who is banging their silverware on the table and the man four tables to the back of me lightly drumming his fingers on the table during his dinner... ALL THIS SENDS ME UP THE WALL....and what can I do? Nothing.

Except remove myself from it all. I have left a buggy FULL of items in a store just because I could no longer take the sounds of certain things happening around me, or ACROSS the store. But music soothes me...I like it soft or loud, it doesn't matter...I think it helps drown everything else out to a certain extent. Things are worse when we are emotionally connected to someone (the snoring, eating, etc...it's all AMPLIFIED). The part I hate the most is that it's annoying...not only to me but my REACTIONS are annoying to them and myself as well.

Collette's Story: I've had it for a while to some extent but its got a lot worse now that I sit next to somebody at work that chews with his mouth open and slurps his coffee. The rage and panic really hits me and now it's started to happen when I see him pull anything out of his bag. My heart starts racing, there's immense pressure in my ears, my teeth grit, my tears well up and I have to hide my mouth so others can't see my expression, I can't' concentrate whatsoever (if my boyfriend crunches toast next to me I have trouble finishing a sentence - I lose my train of thought and then I can't pick it up again - it's literally like I can't think). At work it is embarrassing because it is hard to hide. I know it's showing on my face and my body goes very stiff. Sometimes I type slightly louder in the hope it will drown out the sound but I realized other people notice this and I was embarrassed.

When I'm at home and this happens I sometimes just let myself give up. I squeeze my eyes shut, clasp my hands over my ears and just concentrate on slowing down my breathing and trying to calm down. It's embarrassing enough having a mental health disorder (anxiety in my case) without having something so obvious as a symptom (Im assuming its a symptom in my case). I really look like I'm mental! I've found deep breathing when the sound is going to start helps and trying to relax my shoulders. i try my best to concentrate on that. It's probably not a good idea to leave the room or anything (I do this sometimes) because you'll get used to that avoidance. The only way to get used to it is to expose yourself to it, I reckon.

Will's Story: Other people eating crispy food raises my blood pressure and makes my heart beat faster. I can't control this. I get flushed in the face and start to feel a rage response. I have been very careful to be polite and respectful at the same time that my blood pressure is pounding and my face is red and eyes are twitching. The next kind of eating is when the person eats something and have their lips closed, but I can hear the slushy eating grinding up the sloshy food with lots of saliva going on in the person's mouth, its as if their entire head is a loudspeaker for what's going on in the mouth, (maybe do to with a deviated septum or over-congested sinus cavity). The person is eating their meal and they don't hear it, but all the in-mouth noises are being radiated out quite loudly. Just thinking about it makes me sick

Patti's Story: I also hate the sound of swallowing (even myself), gum chewing, nail biting, specific words (typically any with harsh B or P sounds), any kind of loud noises or sirens and commercials with alarm clocks going off in them.

Arlene's Story: For many years now, I have wanted to murder someone when they make a lot of noise eating, drinking, burping or sniffing. And especially coughing. I positively can't stand fingers clicking or newspapers rustling, or my daughter cracking her knuckles! I can't tolerate cutlery scraping or knocking the sides of the plate. It makes me want to cry just thinking about it. I have often sat next to a big window and wanted to throw my tea cup right through it in a rage because of the noises. I know these noises drive me into an irrational rage and I am really upset and want to run away. It drives me crazy…

Jem's Story: I feel I have a really bad case of this. It started when I was 8 years old and was only breathing and chewing noises nothing else. But as I grew it got rapidly worse. I am now 17 years old and I have to say my teenage life has been nothing but torture. My absolute worse triggers are; chewing, breathing, fans, muffled conversations, lip smacking, flip-flops, dishes clicking together, the letters; s, p, q, k , c and t are so terrible to hear in words when someone speaks. I feel so trapped I didn't ask for this, why me is what I keep asking myself?! I can't bare to talk to my mom because when she talks the saliva and lip smacking she makes my blood boil and my heart literally palpitates. I feel like when I hear a trigger noise I get this flash of shock, fear anxiety and heat from anger. It gets so powerful and those emotions build up so hard that I feel my whole body shaking from rage and then I lose it it my room I have to cry it out for hours.

I honestly can't take it anymore. I tried everything. I tried earplugs but when I put them they help with the chewing/ breathing noises but they increase the muffled noises and conversations trigger that I have, since the plugs are making everything muffled. They only cause another trigger. The only thing that helped somewhat is my mp3 player but its not the best way to cope because I get really bad reactions between songs when there is that little pause where I can hear all the noises.

If I could stop this from continuing believe me I would pay anything to get it fixed. I would never make this up! I'm not sure how to live I can't stop crying. I feel impulses to bawl me eyes out when I hear a trigger. As I flee and get to my room (which is where I go to escape) I hear three more trigger noises. I feel so trapped and overwhelmed I wish I was deaf or dead. But I'm really confusing myself because I am so upset about the thought of dying. I truly wish I could of had a normal life.

Stories about visual triggers

Daryl's Story: Almost any oscillatory, repetitive motion someone does angers me. When I'm in a book store in front of a row of books and out of the corner of my eye I see someone who's sitting in a chair and bouncing their leg up and down, I hate it. Or I'm in my car at a stop light and the women in front of me is repetitively curling a length of her hair around her finger, over and over and over again, I can't stand it a have to look away. Noise and clatter in general now puts me on edge to the extreme. [It feels to me as if there's literally a physical nerve path in my brain that's burned into place and somehow all these stimuli find their way onto this burned in path that goes straight to my centers for rage.]

## Stories about family members who also have the disorder

Kelsey's story: My father is now deceased, but I suspect he had it too, due to his strict manners at the dinner table and his complaints about the sounds that irritated him when I was growing up

Carla's story: My husband of almost 24 years has struggled with this since he was a young boy. One of our daughters has inherited this, onset was later for her, but symptoms just as real. (my mother in law, her mother, and her father have/had it! Back to husband's Great Grandfather!)

Mia's story: i've been super-sensitive to low to medium volume repetitive noises, usually coming from the body (mouth, nose, feet) ever since I can remember. I have felt bad for suddenly literally growling at my boyfriend for "breathing too loud!" or his constant sinus problem! But I can't help it! I believe my sister and father have this annoyance too. It's the only thing we have in common.

Darnell's story: As a child I was beaten for even looking like I was about to burst with rage: my father had [it] and the shrink-people said it was learned behavior. My mother hated me because I hated her sounds. So the cycle might continue except I chose to not have children but my brother did and half of them have [it].

Mike's story: My mother has this syndrome as well, it will be nice to tell her what I've found out and that we're not actually crazy.

Stacey's story: my Dad was in the Army and he would always ridicule us as children and teens for our eating habits. We would not eat with our mouths open, however when we ate something like an apple or chips..the noise of those foods in our mouths used to make my Father cringe. I now find myself with the same problem as my Father.

Gill's story: My sisters, Mother and I ALL share in this same phobia. I prefer to live alone because I can NOT tolerate the noise of others eating. Expecially hard products like pretzels or chips.

# CHAPTER 3
## All about Triggers

We can think of this particular syndrome as a series of uncontrolled, spontaneous reactions to a host of triggers, with the hallmark trigger being an auditory stimulus. What is a trigger? Are the triggers the same for everyone or is there a range of triggers that people have in common? Are there different reactions to the same trigger? Does it matter who or what is making the trigger?

One medical definition of trigger is a substance, object, or agent that initiates or stimulates an action.[1] Another use of the word is to describe a phenomenon that leads to an action or emotional state that activates an underlying brain disorder. In "Sound-Rage" a trigger is a sound, visual, or olfactory phenomenon that stimulates a heightened emotional state associated with physiological changes. A phenomenon can also be described as a sensation, such as someone's hand too close to your face or someone tapping the leg of your chair.

Auditory triggers as "noise"
Sufferers more often than not refer to their triggers as noise, so it is important to distinguish between sound and noise, and what is different between noise as defined by sufferers of this syndrome and noise as defined by the general population.

According to the Canadian Centre for Occupational Health and Safety, sound is what we hear; noise is unwanted sound.[2] The difference between the two is subjective, depending on an individual's likes/dislikes, tolerance, and preferences. More often than not, people call something "noise" depending solely on how loud the sound is. Noise is auditory phenomenon based on its decibel level. Often, ambient or background sound is unnoticeable until its decibel level becomes too great, at which point we call it noise. Here is a typical example: the ambient sound at a restaurant becomes noise when other peoples' conversations and the music coming from speakers mounted on the walls interfere with our ability to hear our dining companions.

Noise exposure, defined as exposure to extremely loud sound, is a known hazard and there are regulations/guidelines with regards to how loud noise can be in transportation and industry, among other places. Hearing loss is a major concern, as is loss of productivity when workers complain they cannot focus on their tasks because of loud, ambient noise. In the general population, noise has an impact on daily living. Its effect can be divided into two categories, physiological and performance. "Suspected effects include cardiovascular function, like hypertension, changes to blood pressure and/or heart rate, and changes in breathing, annoyance, sleeping problems, physical health and mental health. This wide range of effects has led researchers to believe that noise has the ability to act as a general, non-specific stressor."[3]

In "Misophonia" or "Sound-Rage" noise is not a function of decibel level or sensitivity to the loudness of a sound. People with the disorder may have perfect hearing. In fact, based on testimonies, many of the sounds that are triggers are soft sounds like the sound "puh" of "P," the hard "Cuh" of "C," and the sibilant "ssss" of "S." When a sufferer yells, "Stop chewing so loud!" they are more likely referring to the sound itself rather than its decibel level. When a sufferer is subjected to an auditory trigger, it becomes a focal point. The loudness is not in decibels—it is actually a description of how the noise has become the primary sound that the brain is focusing on. The brain hears that sound above and beyond any other.

What does a trigger response feel like?
A trigger elicits behavioral, psychological, and physiological responses. When a person who suffers from "Sound-Rage" hears/sees/senses a trigger, more often than not (s)he describes the feeling of "fight or flight," with flight being the expressed behaviour in this syndrome. The physiological state is associated with the biological changes that arise with a flight response to a stimulus, although the stimulus is neither life threatening nor damaging.

There are no scientific studies that verify the physiological state of a sufferer who is deeply affected by a "Sound-Rage" trigger. The assumption is that the sufferer actually experiences the physical changes associated with flight aspects of the "fight/flight" response and this assumption itself has validity. Self-report measures of stress stack up well against neuro-physiological indices. "In fact, under many circumstances, self-report measures are to be preferred because of their greater face validity and reliability."[4]

The stimulus is perceived by the brain as a threat/danger. It is hypothesized in this primer that the brain misinterprets the stimuli signals as affective pain (not the actual sensation of pain) and it is pain that elicits the immediate, autonomic flight response. Pain and its impact on sufferers are discussed in detail in Chapter 12.

Critically, it is the emotional response of anger that distinguishes this syndrome from fear-based anxiety disorders.[See note 1] This disorder is unique in that anger exists without overt acts of aggression. Accompanying the anger are immediate, autonomic physiological changes associated with flight. The fleeing behavior is hard-wired into our brains. Dating back to the beginning of human history, flight is designed to protect us from harm. When faced with danger, the intense stress response is instinctive. In "Sound-Rage" auditory, visual, and sensory triggers are stressors that are not life-threatening but are nevertheless neurologically perceived as life threatening.[See note 2] It is a complicated, systemic response. Here is a very basic play by play of what happens in the body:

1) When our senses perceive a danger or threat, sensory nerve cells pass the perception of the threat to the hypothalamus area in the brain.
2) Some hypothalamic cells release coricotropin-releasing hormone into the pituitary gland, while other cells simultaneously transmit a nerve signal down the spinal cord and activate the sympathetic motor system.
3) The pituitary in turn incites cells to release a chemical messenger into the bloodstream.
4) Both the chemical messenger and nerve impulse travel to the same destination, the adrenal gland.
6) The adrenal glands sit atop the kidneys. They receive nerve and chemical signals which activate the release of epinephrine (adrenaline) and norepinephrine (noradrenaline) into the bloodstream.
7) These "stress hormones" cause several changes in the body, including an increase in heart rate and blood pressure. Cortisol is

released into the blood stream resulting in an increase in blood pressure, increase in blood sugar levels, and suppression of the immune system.

8) In the lungs, epinephrine binds to receptors on smooth muscle cells wrapped around the bronchioles, causing the muscles to relax and allowing more oxygen into the blood.

9) An increase in heart rate pushes more blood throughout the entire body to deliver oxygen, fuel, and strength to organs and muscles.

10) The brain is directed to focus only on the big picture in order to determine where threat is coming from. Thus, there is trouble focusing on small tasks.

With flight comes emotional and cognitive (thought) reactions to triggers. The prevalent emotional reaction is anger; other emotions, as expressed through testimonies, are upset, sadness, disgust, fear, anxiety, and an overwhelming need to cry. Each emotional feeling has its own range of intensity from mild to strong. Intensity may vary based on the trigger itself, the sufferer's relationship to the trigger, the source of the trigger, and the general stress level of the sufferer. For example, anger ranges from mild annoyance to infuriating rage, with rage being the predominantly noted intensity level.

In addition to physical and emotional reactions, cognition plays a significant role in the response to triggers. Cognition refers to information processing, utilizing mental processes of attention, memory, problem solving, making judgments, and decision making. A sufferer may feel intense hatred toward the origin of the trigger (the source). A cognitive judgment that might arise would be "That person is a slob. People who chew gum are like cows chewing cud." Consistently across testimonies, as story tellers recount their experiences, it is their thoughts about the people creating the triggers—and not the triggers themselves—that illicit negative value judgments. There may be fantasies of harming the person. More often than not, the sufferer believes that the person making the noise is purposely and consciously causing discomfort.

An interesting response reported by some sufferers is mimicking or imitating the sound. This behaviour, which can be perceived as "mocking" by non-sufferers, is often wrongly characterized as echolalia. Echolalia refers to how autistic children process language and communication and is used to describe the echoing or repeating of words and conversations.[See note 3] Mimicry is an automatic, non-conscious, and social phenomenon. It has a palliative aspect, that is, mimicry makes the sufferer feel better. The act of mimicry elicits compassion and empathy, which ameliorates and lessens hostility, competition, and opposition. There is a biological basis for how mimicry reduces the suffering from a trigger, and this is discussed in Chapter 12.

How does a trigger work?
There are no studies addressing the flight response to non-threatening auditory, visual, and sensory triggers in the context of this disorder. The fight/flight response is well described by the literature as it relates to fear of threat or danger. Since fear is not the driver in the disorder, it is uncertain if the same parts of the brain and the same neural processes are in play.

Two of the key goals of this primer are to bring to light how the brain processes sensory information, and to offer possibilities regarding where these processes go awry. Unquestionably, there exist neurological explanations for the responses to the triggers and the expansion of triggers. Responses are non-learned (automatic) and become exacerbated through time by both neurological and cognitive processes that expand the number and kinds of triggers. There may be a neurochemical component that has an impact on the firing of neural signals. The brain is extremely complex: there are many possibilities for how the brain can misfire. The brain regions implicated in trigger stimuli evaluation regarding emotion regulation and modulation, sensory processing, and the integration of cognition (thought), autonomic responses, and sensory information processing are addressed in Chapters 6 though 9.

What are the triggers?
Auditory triggers precede visual ones. Typical triggers include auditory triggers associated with eating; auditory triggers associated with non-chewing sounds from the mouth; auditory nose sounds; auditory body sounds; auditory, repetitive sounds made by people; auditory, repetitive sounds, other; auditory, machine-made sounds; auditory animal sounds; visual triggers; other triggers. Over one

hundred different triggers have been identified; annotated lists are presented in the notes section and by no means exhaustive. See note 4

The number and type of triggers increase through time. This is due to the nature of sensory processing: there is great overlap in the sensory cortices of the brain. The signals from a trigger from one sensory modality (such as a chewing sound) get neurologically associated with signals from another trigger (such as the sight of a person chewing) in a non-conscious, non-learned process. Cognitive processes whereby the brain learns associations also contribute to the expansion of triggers. The expansion of triggers and related aspects are discussed in detail in Chapter 16.

<u>Are there commonalities in the triggers?</u>
A cognitive behavior therapist once remarked to me that the triggers are "all over the place." Nevertheless, there appear to be some commonalities threaded throughout a large number of triggers. The primary commonality is the repetitive nature of a number of auditory triggers such as consistent dog barking, repeated clicking on a keyboard, or repeated pops from a gum chewer. It may be that it takes more than one exposure to an auditory trigger to stimulate firing of the neurons alerting the system to danger. Similarly, visual triggers such as shaking legs might require a certain amount of time before the neurons are alerted to danger. The brain itself might be waiting for verification: one or two incidences of the trigger might put the system on alert, initiating selective attention. Once there are a certain repetitions, the brain signals danger.

<u>Does the origin of the trigger matter?</u>
> *Strangers vs. Friend. Whether the noise is made by someone who's "one of us" (friend who cares about my welfare) or "one of them" (stranger, neighbor I have no special connection with, indifferent to my welfare) is a big factor. I used to go to Burningman and the first 3 days were full of banging and construction as people got their camps put up. It was a sea of sound in a community of choice, and I felt surrounded by community, so it was OK – even a vital part of the experience.[5]*

The origin of the trigger plays a role in the syndrome. Who (or what) is making the sound or presenting the visual can mean the difference between a non-response and a physiological response accompanied by intense emotion. It varies with each individual and may be correlated with the length of time the sufferer has had the disorder. For many, family members are the source of the triggers; for others, it is the stranger chewing gum on the train. Someone with the disorder can have a symptom-free outing with a friend who is chewing gum and might go into immediate reactive mode when a stranger who walks by is sniffing. The source of the trigger as a component of how different stimuli are assessed by the brain is addressed in Chapter 15.

# CHAPTER 4
## Do I Have this Syndrome?

*I would have no clue whether or not I suffer from this, but it does provide a neat explanation for:*

- *Glaring with rage at my aunt across the table when I was, oh, 8 or 9, asking her to shut her mouth while she chews (I promise I wasn't a devil child otherwise!!)*
- *Switching from mild-mannered, polite student to evil, death-ray-eyed monster when students in the library slobbered on hard candy, sniffed one time too many, rustled their papers, or creaked in their seats*
- *Running over to my boyfriend to hold his leg still when I hear it repeatedly tapping against his pants.[1]*

As humans, we are increasingly and consciously interested in understanding our inner lives and our physical bodies. We not only want to identify our symptoms, we want to understand our symptoms. Our problem-solving self wants to identify causes and to define what is causing us pain. Repeatedly, sufferers and their care givers ask, "What is wrong with me? Is this what I have?"

The following survey serves to help identify if "Sound-Rage" or "Misophonia" describes your experience. Please note this disclaimer: this is neither a scientific survey nor a rigorously validated survey. It bears no relation to a medical or psychiatric protocol for diagnosis. It is simply a descriptor of the symptoms, which may or may not help you identify your particular health issue.

<u>Onset</u>
My rage reactions built up through time. At first, the sounds were just annoying.

1) True
2) False

*Do I have this syndrome?* The initial onset of the syndrome is sudden, i.e., it simply shows up. There is no eventual build-up.
Through time, other triggers that were annoying may become significant, but the onset of the actual disorder itself is not gradual. The first experience with reacting strongly to sounds is often remembered as something significant and new.

Age of onset
I first noticed that certain sounds disturbed me

1) before age 5
2) age 5-10
3) age 11-15
4) age 16-20
5) age 20 and greater

*Do I have this syndrome?* Based on the biographies and testimonies taken from personal communication, interviews, and from pubic websites, the range of age of onset tends to be between the ages of 8 and 13. There have been accounts of age of onset in early childhood, early teen years, and several reports of an adult onset (age 18 or greater). As a rule, the onset of the disorder is late childhood through middle adolescence.

First triggers
The first people whose noises bothered me were

1) close family member—mother or father
2) close family member—sibling, other family member living with me
3) a friend or acquaintance
4) classmate or teacher
5) a stranger

*Do I have this syndrome?* Typically, the first person to be the source of a trigger is the mother or father, followed by close family members. While it is rare that the first people whose noises triggered a reaction were strangers, it is not impossible.

The first trigger to disturb me was

1) chewing food—eating
2) chewing gum
3) breathing sounds or other sounds from the mouth
4) other sounds like the ticking of a clock
5) a visual—such as someone swinging their legs

*Do I have this syndrome?* Typically, the first trigger is associated with eating. Gum chewing, breathing sounds, and other sounds such as sniffing and snoring associated with the mouth and nose are also among the first triggers.

Noticing a trigger
When I notice someone near me chewing gum (or food) I

1) focus on the sound and the person and feel annoyed
2) focus on the sound and the person and feel extreme anger
3) focus on the sound and the person and feel anger and the need to flee

*Do I have this syndrome?* People with the disorder not only notice if someone is chewing, but tend to focus on the person and their chewing. They feel physical changes—such as heart speeding up, a sense of nervousness or anxiety, an urgency to flee, an emotion of anger, and quite possibly thoughts of hatred or aggression.

Type of reaction to triggers
My reaction to one or more triggers is

1) annoyance
2) annoyance, frustration, sometimes discomfort
3) anxiety, tension. I feel changes in my body, such as heart racing, temperature rising
4) My body changes and I find I cannot focus on the task at hand. I focus on the trigger
5) I feel anger, rage, and/or hatred

*Do I have this syndrome?* The syndrome is characterized by a strong, immediate, and uncontrolled response to chewing. People experience one or a combination of the following: anger, the urge or need to flee, and negative thoughts about the person/object creating the trigger.

I hate loud noises.

1) True
2) False

*Do I have this syndrome?* Hating and responding to loud noises might be a startle response, an indication of a sensory processing disorder, or might be from undue stress. It is not an indication or symptom of the disorder. The vast majority of sufferers have normal hearing.

I am extremely bothered by barking dogs.

1) True
2) False

*Do I have this syndrome?* Many sufferers include barking dogs as one of their triggers. However, there are many people who do not have this syndrome who become highly agitated by barking dogs.

Growth of triggers
As I get older, my list of triggers (stressors that make me feel the flight response) has grown from eating/chewing sounds to include other oral (mouth) sounds such as snoring or sniffing.

1) True
2) False

As I get older, my list of triggers (stressors that make me feel the flight response) has grown from "mouth/nose" sounds to include other sounds such as clocks ticking, dogs barking, finger tapping on a computer keyboard etc.

1) True
2) False

As I get older, my list of triggers (stressors that make me feel the flight response) has grown from sounds to include visual triggers, like someone pointing or someone swinging their legs.

1) True
2) False

As I get older, my list of triggers (stressors that make me feel the flight response) has grown to include certain odors.

1) True
2) False

*Do I have this syndrome?* Sufferers report that the range of triggers grows through time and the types of triggers also change and magnify.

I find that at times if I know where the sound is coming from, it might not bother me. For example, if I thought the cracking sound was from someone chewing gum, but it turns out to be from something totally different, my physiological and emotional response stops.

1) True
2) False

*Do I have this syndrome?* Sufferers report that knowing who or where the trigger is coming sometimes changes the response to the trigger.

My reaction to sounds and other stimuli:

1) Has had little, if any, impact on my life
2) Has caused me to alter my life style

3) Has caused difficulties in work relationships
4) Has caused difficulties in personal relationships
5) Has lowered the overall quality of my life

*Do I have this syndrome?* Almost universally, sufferers report an overall diminished quality of life due to impaired relationships with friends, family, and co-workers. Many testimonies suggest changes in life style, from not using public transportation or going to movies, to the inability to work or visit public places.

Obsessive Thoughts
I have obsessive thoughts about people eating and/or other things

1) True
2) False

*Do I have this syndrome?* There is no evidence, medical or otherwise, to indicate that obsessive thoughts are part of the syndrome. While there is the possibility that some people also experience Obsessive Compulsive Disorder (OCD), "Sound-Rage" and OCD are separate and distinct syndromes. In other words, having OCD does not imply that you have "Sound-Rage." Conversely, having "Misophonia" does not imply that you have OCD. Hypervigilance, an enhanced or exaggerated scanning of the environment for threat, is a common component of "Misophonia" that is often mistakenly confused with obsessive behavior.

# CHAPTER 5
## What's the Diagnosis?

*I have tried to get help for this since I started therapy in 1987. If I did nothing about my problem and just expected everyone to change for me I could understand how that could seem rude. I have tried to get rid of my fear for 20 years. I have done every kind of counseling and therapy (from group to individual, meditation, etc.). The psychiatrists and therapists that I have encountered over all these years have never been able to help me with this and haven't heard of anything as extreme as my problem is. I'm wondering if anyone else feels like I do and if anyone has ever gotten any relief.[1]*

*I can not eat around my family and have great anxiety about going into stores because I know I will hear something that bothers me. Most people will say to "Just ignore it" and I have to say this is infuriating. These sounds produce a true physiological response (stomach in knots, heart racing) as well as a psychological response (anger or even rage, anxiety, depression, helplessness). I have been to countless therapists, although no one knows how to help me.[2]*

*We have been visiting health professionals here for nearly 4 years. Our Doctor just thought [our son] was naughty and would grow out of this. Then we kept saying it was noise that caused all of his problems so we were sent to an Audiologist, She diagnosed Tinnitus and sent us to see a Tinnitus retraining Therapist. After about 2 sessions she realized that [our son] did not have conventional tinnitus. All of this time I kept telling these professionals to look at Misophonia - but it was only last month that we got a psychiatrist to diagnose this condition.[3]*

*I stayed up for hours last night searching the internet (yet again) trying to figure out what is going on with [my daughter]. For at least 9-10 months now, things have been bothering her, and it's getting worse... It seems there are more and more triggers, and her responses come across as totally irrational... With her intolerance (sp) of certain sounds, her anger and compulsion to react, the fact this is getting worse, from what I've read, it all fits. My question is, how do I find someone to properly diagnose and help her.*[4]

This is a syndrome unlike all others. There is powerful anger, yet little overt aggression and virtually no physical violence or harm. There is extreme hatred, yet the hatred is uncharacteristically different from the conventional wisdom that holds that hatred comprises memory, value judgment, and cognitive associations. Here it is immediate, reactive, and dissipates within seconds as if someone turned on and off a "hatred button." There is anxiety—but anxiety is only one of part of the emotional equation and is more likely a consequence of the disorder rather than a cause or correlate.

Conventional pharmacology—medication routinely given for anxiety, panic, and depression—does not alter the reaction to triggers, suggesting that there are neurological and neurochemical processes that have not yet been identified by the scientific and medical communities. The number, kinds, and sources of triggers actually increase through time. There is a reaction to hearing certain sounds but to some extent the reaction depends on who or what is creating the trigger. This suggests that it is not necessarily the sound itself but the sounds in context, suggesting some cognitive (thought) processes come into play.

With cognitive, physiological, and neurological components interacting in ways that are complex, vague, and barely understood, it is virtually impossible to make a diagnosis based on known disorders. Trying to match this syndrome to another is a bit like trying to fit a square peg into a round hole.

Is this a mental disorder?

The classification of mental disorders is known as psychiatric nosology or taxonomy. Currently, there are currently two widely established systems for classifying mental disorders: The World Health Organization's International Classification of Diseases (ICD-10), Chapter V and the American Psychiatric Association's (APA) *Diagnostic and Statistical Manual of Mental Disorders,* fourth edition, text revision (DSM IV-TR).

Unrecognized and unnamed, examination of "Sound-Rage" or "Misophonia" is in its infancy. Like other syndromes before it, there is an evolution of discovery born from a process of describing, theorizing, testing, and verifying. The DSM IV-TR defines a mental disorder as "a clinically significant behavioral or psychological syndrome or pattern that occurs in an individual and that is associated with present distress (a painful symptom) or disability (impairment in one or more important areas of functioning) or with a significantly increased risk of suffering death, pain or disability."[See note 1] Based on this definition, "Sound-Rage" is a mental disorder.

Is this a mental disorder that arises from physiological or neurological dysfunction? Is the rage a learned response or is it a reaction that is derived from a brain malfunction? Or is it a neurological disorder with co-occurring psychological disorders? Tourette Syndrome (TS) provides an interesting history with aspects that are strikingly similar and can help put into perspective how information is key to diagnosis, prognosis, and ultimately appropriate therapies.

TS is an inherited, genetically determined, neurological disorder. While its exact impact on the world's population is not known, it is estimated to affect between 100,000 to 300,000 people in the U.S. alone. Onset tends to be abrupt—for example, vocal tics begin as if out of nowhere—and usually begins with simple tics that progress to more complex tics through time. Onset occurs by the age of thirteen with an average onset around age nine. It is characterized by vocal tics—grunts, "barking," and other involuntary sounds—and motor tics, such as facial grimacing, blinking, hand, and shoulder jerking. There are some occurrences of spitting and echolalia and, rarely, coprolalia (explosive involuntary cursing).

The pathology of TS is not well understood, but scientific study has uncovered both neurological and chemical abnormalities. It is widely believed that there are abnormalities in brain neurochemistry where dopamine neurotransmission play a role and abnormality in the brain's basal ganglia circuitry. The current conceptualization of the syndrome focuses on how it is a neurological disorder with common psychiatric problems based on family genetic studies.[5]

Co-occurring psychiatric problems include attention deficit disorder (ADD), obsessive-compulsive disorder (OCD), and opposition defiance disorder (ODD). While identifying the genetic variants contributing to TS susceptibility has proven difficult, research has found neural circuits connecting TS and OCD at the frontal cortico-basal ganglia.[6] Pharmacologically, there is a menu of medications that modulate the tics. Comprehensive Behavioral Intervention for Tics (CBIT) is a therapeutic technique that combines elements of habit reversal training with function-based behavioral interventions and psychoeducation. However, despite the current state of knowledge, people throughout the world are still misdiagnosed as having nervous habits or attention-getting behaviors.

The first reported case in medical literature was in 1825 which described noblewoman Marquise de Dampierre with symptoms of coprolalia. Sixty years later, Dr. George Gilles de la Tourette described nine patients with "maladie des tics." For the next eighty or so years, people continued to believe that the barking sounds, sniffing, eye blinking, and assorted repetitive motor movements were psychological. They attributed TS to such things as sudden violent psychic anxiety, trauma, alcoholism, and brain lesions.

In the mid-1900's, theorists continued the belief that TS was psychogenic, that is, having a psychological rather than physical cause, based primarily on inferences about behavior rather than on empirical evidence. In analyzing behavior rather than the underlying neurobiology, tics were seen as expressions of emotional conflicts. It seemed logical and reasonable to theorize that if a person started "barking" or making funny noises they were expressing anger at the people around them. If a student exhibited motor tics in class they were considered frustrated, displaying aggression, and/or acting out from insecurity.

As early as 1948 and as late as 1961, several psychiatrists theorized that Tourette was a response to at least one domineering parent and was an expression against authority.[7] In the 1960s, drugs called neuroleptics were found to be effective in treating the motor aspects, and this refocused attention from a psychological to an organic central nervous system cause.[8]

The history of Tourette demonstrates the progression of thought from a psychological disorder to an organic one. It also aptly illustrates the ease and danger of ascribing psychological explanations in the absence of neurological data. "Barking" tourettic children were once thought to be acting out aggression, vocally manifesting their hostility. It would be very easy to create similar explanations or stories that would logically accommodate observed anger and hatred responses to stimuli.

Is this a neurological disorder?
Is "Sound-Rage" a learned, emotional response to environmental conditions or is it a neurological dysfunction? It seems highly unlikely that the response to triggers is learned. From a statistical perspective, disparate populations of people having the same syndrome characteristics such as age of onset, abruptness of onset, and unique physiological response of anger without overt aggression is not coincidence.

Is this something one has at birth? In their quest for understanding, sufferers have attempted to analyze their reactions step by step and to marry their anger reactions to situations and dynamics of their childhood. These analyses might or might not have any validity. They might or might not make sense. Often, in re-creating childhood, we create new stories of what was. These stories rarely help overcome symptoms and rarely create effective strategies for dealing with pain and suffering. They are not conducive to creating new ways of communicating needs or new ways to think about the disorder. What these analyses provide, however, is insight into the emotional environment in which sufferers first had onset of symptoms. It might well be that a turmoiled and harsh environment created the stressors which precipitated the onset.

There exists a strong possibility that there is a hereditary component to the disorder, i.e., a person is born with the genetic make-up to manifest the disorder. Presently, no data exist to indicate whether or not the disorder runs in families. However, based on testimonies and personal communication, there seems to be a subset of sufferers who have family members with the same condition.

While the predisposition for the disorder is most likely present at birth, its onset is determined by a combination of genetic and environmental factors. Environmental factors such as undue stress may precipitate the chain of events that lead to the disorder's onset. Many sufferers report dysfunction and stress in their home environments when they were young. On the other hand, it may be that the disorder is latent; it is genetically determined at birth and will manifest regardless of external or environmental factors.

If a person has this from birth, why doesn't it appear until later in childhood? Like other neurological disorders that have an onset in childhood or adolescence, such as Tourette syndrome, it does not manifest until the brain has undergone certain changes. What are these changes? At the present time, there are no studies at all on "Sound-Rage" and thus no studies whatsoever on its etiology or cause. An onset that does not occur at birth suggests that there are developmental events that must occur prior to the appearance of the first symptom. These developments may be neurochemical (a change in brain chemistry) or neurobiological (a change in the nervous system).

One might speculate that there is a dysfunction in the developmental of neural pathways, the wiring of a brain structure. The brain undergoes changes throughout life. One era of rapid change is during adolescence when there is a major reduction in the number of synapses. This reduction is thought to be a "pruning." Unused synaptic connections are removed, presumably leaving a brain that operates faster and is more efficient. Broad cortical regions are activated in younger children and pruning might permit reactions to stimuli to become more selective. From the ages of 7 though 16, there are also other changes. There are developmental increases in amygdala–prefrontal cortex connectivity, alterations in amygdala activation, and changes in the processing of emotional and stressful stimuli.[9]

Is this an anxiety disorder?
The word anxiety comes from LATIN *ānxius* which was derived from *angere*, meaning to torment, strangle, distress. It is a state of being, comprising physiological and psychological components. These components are cognitive (thoughts), behavioral, somatic (bodily, physical) and emotional. Common physiological symptoms may include changes in body temperature like sweating or getting shivers, queasiness, and increase in heart rate. Cognitive symptoms include having "what- if thoughts" or catastrophic thoughts—ideas of bad things that might or might not happen in the near future. In general, when people say they feel anxious or anxiety, they are describing a conglomerate of feelings, including worry, apprehension, uneasiness, and dread.

Having anxiety in and of itself does not constitute having a disorder. Insurance companies code anxiety as a way or state of being as opposed to defining it as a disorder. They consider it an unpleasant, but not necessarily pathological, emotional state resulting from an unfounded or irrational perception of danger.[See note 2] Some anxiety is considered a normal reaction to the vagaries of life. There are schools of thought that some anxiety operates as a motivator, helping to achieve or move towards accomplishing goals.

It is a candidate for being classified as a disorder when it becomes overwhelming and interferes with everyday life. Anxiety disorders have explicitly been defined: as outlined in the DSM IV- TR, anxiety disorders include generalized anxiety disorder (GAD), social anxiety disorder (also known as social phobia), specific phobia, panic disorder with and without agoraphobia, obsessive-compulsive disorder (OCD), posttraumatic stress disorder (PTSD), anxiety secondary to medical condition, acute stress disorder (ASD), and substance-induced anxiety disorder. Since sufferers have been misdiagnosed as having a phobia and/or OCD, or suffering from post traumatic stress disorder, a closer look at these classified anxiety disorders will help determine if they approximate "Misophonia."

Is this a phobia?
*I also have this phobia for about 5 years. DO NOT*

*WAIT FOR IT TO GET BETTER ON ITS OWN. MOST TIMES IT WILL NOT! Don't suffer in silence people! I'm fed up with people giving advice like "ignore it" or "remove yourself from the situation" You can't run away from it, it will always be there!*[10]

The media[See note 3] and some mental health providers have labeled the syndrome a phobia. The DSM IV-TR Criteria for Specific Phobia[11] are:

- Persistent fear that is excessive or unreasonable, cued by the presence or anticipation of a specific object or situation.
- Exposure provokes immediate anxiety, which can take the form of a situationally predisposed panic attack.
- Patients recognize that the fear is excessive or unreasonable.
- Patients avoid the phobic situation or else endure it with intense anxiety or distress.
- The distress in the feared situation interferes significantly with the person's normal routine, occupational functioning, or social activities or relationships.
- In persons younger than 18 years, the duration is at least 6 months.
- The fear is not better accounted for by another mental disorder.

When people describe their disorder, the one word that is either downplayed or missing from the dialogue is fear. Fear is a lynchpin in phobias. But are people with "Misophonia" or "Sound-Rage" afraid of chewing sounds? Do they feel fear when they seeing a swinging leg? When confronted by a strong unpleasant odor, do they identify fear as their immediate, prevalent feeling or thought?

A person who is claustrophobic is terrified of being in closed-in, small spaces. The fear is specific and defined. As a claustrophobic approaches an elevator, the idea of being in it may induce immediate fear. In the disorder "Misophonia" the thought of hearing a trigger or seeing a trigger does not produce fear. When in the presence of a trigger, the first and foremost emotional response is anger. The anticipation of hearing/seeing a trigger does not produce the rage/hatred response, although it may induce anticipatory anxiety.

People with phobias have a physiological response when confronted by their target phobia: panic. A panic attack has been said to be one of the most intensely frightening, upsetting and uncomfortable experiences of a person's life and it may take days to initially recover from it. Many who experience a panic attack for the first time fear they are having a heart attack or a nervous breakdown.

By way of comparison, a person who hears someone chewing gum will have a physiological response of associated with identifying danger: flight. And as soon as the trigger is gone, so is the overwhelming physiological response. Most telling is the ineffectiveness of phobia therapies on mitigating the autonomic response to certain trigger stimuli. Phobia treatment includes exposure, which is an ineffective therapy for "Sound-Rage." In fact, exposure can lead to extreme negative responses. Exposure therapy is addressed in greater detail in Chapters 12 and 17.

Is this obsessive compulsive disorder (OCD)?
OCD typically manifests itself as an array of elaborated intrusive thoughts of images (obsessions). These are accompanied by ritualized, over, or covert behaviors (compulsions) that individuals feel compelled to perform. The DSM IV-TR criteria for OCD states:

- At some point during the course of the disorder, the person has recognized that the obsessions or compulsions are excessive or unreasonable.
- The obsessions or compulsions cause marked distress, take up more than 1 hour a day, or significantly interfere with the person's normal routine, occupation, or usual social activities.
- If another Axis I disorder, substance use, or general medical condition is present, the content of the obsessions or compulsions is not restricted to it.

The DSM IV-TR Criteria for Obsessive-Compulsive Disorder, Obsessions are:
- Recurrent and persistent thoughts, impulses, or images that are experienced as intrusive and inappropriate, causing anxiety or distress.
- The thoughts, impulses, or images are not simply excessive worries about real-life problems.

- The person attempts to ignore or suppress such thoughts, impulses, or images or to neutralize them with some other thought or action.
- The person recognizes that the obsessional thoughts, impulses, or images are a product of his or her own mind.

The DSM IV-TR Criteria for Obsessive-Compulsive Disorder, Compulsions are:
- Repetitive behaviors or mental acts that the person feels driven to perform in response to an obsession or according to rules that must be applied rigidly.
- The behaviors or mental acts are aimed at preventing or reducing distress or preventing some dreaded event or situation.
- These behaviors or mental acts either are not connected in a realistic way with what they are designed to neutralize or prevent, or they are clearly excessive.

The main factor that distinguishes OCD from "Sound-Rage" is that obsessions and compulsions can and do exist without external stimuli (or environmental situations) to trigger the thoughts. In "Sound-Rage" an anger response requires a trigger. In fact, "Sound-Rage" is predicated on reaction to external stimuli.

Nevertheless, people with "Sound-Rage" are diagnosed as having OCD most likely because their perseveration (for example, the inability to switch ideas about something) and rampant, premonitory anxiety associated with being confronted by a trigger are misinterpreted as being obsessive. "Sound-Rage" responses may seem like stand-ins for "recurrent and persistent thoughts, impulses, or images" when in actuality, the disorder is about an immediate reaction to a stimulus. Simply thinking about someone chewing may result in premonitory anxiety, but it will not elicit the same anger/rage physical and emotional response. There would be no desperate need to get away because there would be nothing to get away from.

"Misophonia" sufferers spend an inordinate amount of time coping and dealing with triggers. They are very attentive to the environment in which triggers may occur. This attention is referred to as hypervigilance, the brain's way of keeping alert to possible danger or pain. However, many sufferers and the public as well misinterpret hypervigilance as "being obsessive."

Anti-anxiety drugs that help calm OCD do not seem to have any effect on "Sound-Rage." For more on hypervigilance refer to Chapter 14. A thorough analysis of the relevant brain regions, brain circuitry and multi-sensory processing can be found in Chapters 7 through 9.

Is this post traumatic stress disorder (PTSD)?

> *Ever since she was a little girl, mealtime has been a torture for Adah Siganoff. The eating sounds – the chewing, the slurping, the chomping – drove Adah to distraction. She'd spent many years in therapy trying to deal with what had been mistakenly diagnosed as post-traumatic stress.*[12]

Posttraumatic stress disorder (PTSD) is a fairly well documented psychiatric disorder that affects people who have experienced or witnessed a life-threatening event. Traumatic events such as rape, natural disasters (like the flooding and overwhelming destruction caused by tsunamis), and serious car accidents can have a significant impact on a person's long term mental health. It has been theorized that when people who have psychological and physiological vulnerability are exposed to a stressful event, they develop the belief that these stressful events are unpredictable and uncontrollable—and they will become fearful about the repetition of this stress. This leads to a cycle of "chronic overarousal" and "anxious apprehension."

According to the Department of Commerce's National Technical Information Service, as many as 20 million Americans appear to have had at least one lifetime episode of PTSD, making this diagnosis one of the most prevalent of all mental disorders, surpassed by substance use disorders and depression.[13]

A person with PTSD has unexpected reoccurrences of the event; these are episodic "flashbacks" and can cause the person to act as if (s)he is reliving the experience. A color, smell, object, or sound which is similar to or associated with the trauma may trigger intrusive memories resulting in a great deal of emotional pain and distress. A person with PTSD avoids situations or activities that are reminders of the original traumatic event. Often, the sufferer behaves as if his/her life is constantly threatened.[14] The traumas most commonly associated with PTSD among women are rape and sexual molestation, and among men are witnessing and exposure to combat.[15]

PTSD is characterized by a general numbing of general responsiveness; recurring, disturbing memories of the event which push into awareness; intrusive memories; and recurring nightmares about what happened. Other diagnostic symptoms include avoiding stimuli/situations that might be associated with the trauma, increased arousal, difficulty falling asleep, difficulty staying asleep, anger, and hypervigilance.[See note 4] For example, hyper-alertness and sleep disturbances are common among veterans wounded in Vietnam.[16]

Why would someone with a "Sound-Rage" be diagnosed with PTSD? It may be that the practitioner making the diagnosis assumes that there was a traumatic event in the client's life such as a serious accident or child abuse and further assumes that the sound of gum chewing is the trigger for the traumatic event and flashbacks. Superficially, this explanation for observed behaviors seems acceptable, but it is misguided.

PTSD behaviors of increased arousal, anger and hypervigilance look strikingly similar to those of "Sound-Rage." There is looking around to see where the danger is. There is heightened awareness and anxiety. There is marked avoidance of situations where the triggers may occur. And most importantly, both disturbances cause clinically significant distress or impairment in social, occupational, or other important areas of functioning, or impair the individual's ability to pursue some necessary task.

An astute practitioner, however, should be able to see the marked deviations from PTSD. These are: the obvious lack of a significant traumatic event, the lack of nightmares which typify the PTSD sufferer, and a lack of general numbing, among other critical factors.[See note 5]

If this is not OCD, PTSD or a phobia, what exactly is it? Is it an anxiety disorder? Based on a thorough review of the DSM IV-TR, it is not an anxiety disorder. It may be that anxiety is a co-morbid or also-occurring but separate condition. There is no question that anxiety is a close bedfellow, an affect arising as a reaction to or result of the disorder itself. Anxiety is not a driver for the syndrome but it clearly connected to it: there is tremendous anxiety associated with avoiding situations and people aligned with triggers. Many sufferers report feeling anxiety in situations where a trigger might occur.

With respect to medications for anxiety, selective serotonin reuptake inhibitors (SSRIs) have been shown to be the best-tolerated medications. This class of medication includes fluoxetine (Prozac), fluvoxamine (Luvox), citalopram (Celexa), escitalopram (Lexapro), paroxetine (Paxil), and sertraline (Zoloft). They are also effective for panic disorder, OCD, PTSD, social anxiety disorder, and GAD. However, medications used with success on anxiety disorders are not effective for mitigating the impacts of triggers and there is no evidence that SSRI's are palliative.

Nevertheless, the media have played a large role in misdiagnosing and inappropriately diagnosing the syndrome without substantiating evidence. In the summer of 2010, TV and media guru Dr. Phil conducted a brief "sound sensitivity" interview on his "Am I the only One?" segment. He told the woman describing her aversion to sounds, "It's an anxiety response. It is not weird; one thing we know about a sound, if you decide to focus on it you have no control on it. Anxiety arises when we feel out of control. You are going to have to deal with your reaction to the stimulus… you have complete control over your reaction. You need to learn how to calm yourself in the presence of these stimuli. It's very doable with systematic desensitization. Where you have the ability to have amazing control in the presence of these stimuli."

In additional to an incorrect diagnosis, he mistakenly assumes that the sound sensitivity is a type of phobia. "Though some people are paralyzed by a fear for their entire life, the typical time it takes to treat and eliminate a phobia is less than 10 hours. Your fear may have nothing to do with the stimulus that sends your heart racing, so you can slowly learn to confront it and overcome your phobia." [17, See note 6]

## Is this a sensory processing disorder (SPD)?

*I have been told that this is called Sensory Integrative Dysfunction or Sensory Processing Disorder. There is a great deal of variation in symptoms. Any or all of the senses can be affected to varying degrees. Basically, it is the nervous system responding inappropriately to stimuli that wouldn't bother the average person. It doesn't get better on its own, I promise you. It is really hard to avoid people when they eat or chew gum. I've spent a lifetime trying. Get her to a doctor that is familiar with Sensory disorders. (Most of them treat children with ADHD, Autism, PDD-NOS, depression, aggression, and other types of disorders related to a varying inability to appropriately sort sensory stimuli).* [18]

Even though it is discrete and unrelated, it is tempting to call "Sound-Rage" a sensory processing disorder. Auditory (hearing sounds like finger tapping), visual (someone fidgeting and twirling their hair), and olfactory (standing next to someone who is perspiring heavily) senses take in information. The input (information about the stimulus) is processed in the brain. Something goes amiss in the processing. Instead of a "no reaction" to an ambient environmental stimulus there is an emotional reaction. The emotional reaction is one of rage with thoughts of hatred and a physiological response of flight. One could say that the sensory input was processed incorrectly. However, that does not make it a sensory processing disorder.

A "sensory processing disorder" has an entirely different schema. Sensory processing is a difficulty in the brain's ability to integrate information. In its extreme form, when it results in difficulties in daily living, it is considered a disorder, although it is not recognized by the American Psychiatric Association's *Diagnostic and Statistical Manual*. The theory was first addressed by an occupational therapist in the 1970s. Dr. A. Jean Ayres introduced the idea that certain people's brains can't process all the information coming in through the senses to provide a clear picture of what's happening both internally and externally. She further postulated that there are seven, rather than five senses, adding the "internal" senses of body awareness (proprioceptive) and movement (vestibular).

The inability to simultaneously synthesize information is apparent almost from birth. Infants and toddlers with a resistance to cuddling, to the point of arching away when held, may be feeling actual pain when being touched. In pre-school, children who are displaying temper tantrum behaviors may actually be reacting to over-stimulation; fight or flight behaviors may become apparent in elementary school when there is too much stimulation. Sensory processing dysfunction is most apparent as a decreased ability to respond to sensory information in order to behave in a meaningful and consistent way. Developmentally, it leads to difficulty in using sensory information to plan and organize how the body works in relation to the environment and to make sense of the environment.

In her book *Sensational Kids*[19] Miller describes three subsets of sensory processing disorder: Sensory Modulation Disorder (SMD), of which sensory defensiveness is a sub category, Sensory-Based Motor Disorder (SBMD), and Sensory Discrimination Disorder. Sensory defensiveness most closely mirrors "Sound-Rage" and will be addressed for its differences and commonalities.[See note 7]

> When asked about the possibility of a link between "misophonia" and sensory processing disorder, Dr. Schoen, assistant director of Sensory Processing Disorder (SPD) Foundation Research and the clinical services advisor of the STAR Center, responded, "Individuals with sensory processing disorder typically have impairments in more than one sensory system. Clearly the behavioral manifestations of individuals with misophonia appear similar to those with sensory over-responsivity in the auditory domain. At the present time, the biological mechanisms and implicated structures for SPD and misophonia are not well documented and the

*etiologies are unknown. More research is needed to determine the similarities, differences and co-occurrence of the two conditions.*"[20]

Sensory defensiveness, a sub category of sensory modulation disorder, is an over-sensitivity and negatdive reaction to non-aversive tactile, vestibular, auditory, visual, gustatory, olfactory, and proprioceptive sensory input. A walk through a shopping mall can feel like an onslaught and totally alienate, disorient, and disturb the sensory defensive person. Examples of sensory defensiveness are: grass feeling abrasive on the toes, being unable to stand erect on an escalator, jumping at the sudden sound of a siren, being overwhelmed by bright lights.

One theory speculates that in order to modulate sensation for adaptive behavior, there must be an appropriate balance between habituation and sensitization.[21] Habituation occurs when the central nervous system recognizes stimuli as familiar and therefore no longer responds to them. Sensitization is the process in which the central nervous system recognizes stimuli as harmful or important and therefore heightens the response. Thus, the railroad crossing alarm makes a loud sound as a train approaches, but the central nervous systems knows that it is neither harmful or important from six blocks away. Individuals with sensory defensiveness have low thresholds for sensory stimuli—they have heightened responses with less habituation; the train alarm is disturbing even though it is six blocks away.

In her book, *Too Loud, Too Bright, Too Fast, Too Tight,* Sharon Heller discusses the impact of un-modulated sensory receptivity on a person's social, psychological, and emotional life. People who are on constant guard, fighting or fleeing from particular stimuli, are creating battle grounds within their own biological ecosystem. "If one's senses feed ongoing negative information into the limbic channel, the person's emotional voyage is achingly intense and volatile."[22]

Is "Sound-Rage" a subset of sensory defensiveness? Both create sympathetic nervous system arousal, hypervigilance, avoidance, and feelings of a lack of control. Nevertheless, there are many fundamental differences in symptoms, age of onset, and neurobiological processes. A sensory- defensive person's reaction to sound is more likely to be a startle response or a reaction to loud noise; it may result in a flight response but lacks the key emotional response of anger.

What's the diagnosis?

It stands to reason that the current psychiatric literature does not have a known syndrome into which "Sound-Rage" might fall. It is currently an orphan disorder, unclaimed by the medical and psychological communities. Medications that are successful tools in the menu of coping strategies for known anxiety disorders are not palliative (soothing the symptoms of a disorder without effecting a cure) with this disorder. Anti-anxiety medications do help alleviate overall levels of associated anxiety and this in turn might help reduce overall stress. They do have an impact on the immediate physiological and emotional response to stimuli—however, the overall impact of triggers is not diminished. There is no demonstrated reduction in kinds of triggers. They do not alter the ancillary affect of hypervigilance. Based on testimonies, exposure therapy that has practical application with phobias actually exacerbates the symptoms.

One critical fact remains: this disorder may represent an entirely new paradigm of mental disorder.[See note 8]

# CHAPTER 6
## The Brain: Overview

*Your entire sensory apparatus is there to make successful representations of the outside world. The goal of sensory processing is to take a signal, like a sound or a vision, from your environment and use it to drive behavior. The brain needs to recognize and learn about these inputs in order to survive.*[1]

*You maybe can learn to calm yourself down after the fact, but even after working on this over time, the initial reaction is the same. It's like our brain is wired that way.*[2]

Introduction
Let's think about the ocean. The ocean supports many interconnected ecosystems, where a change in one part of the world's ocean will have an impact clear across earth. Way down in its depths live mysterious, rare, and unique creatures whose biology seems to come from another galaxy. We can picture it. We can conjure up the sounds and smells of the beach. And yet, when we ask ourselves about how the ocean works, how its tides and currents flow across the planet, we aren't necessarily clear about the answers. The oceans influence our daily lives through weather patterns, the food it offers us, and its potential for inundating an entire coastal community. It remains largely unexplored and relatively unknown, despite its importance to how we live our lives.

So, too, the brain. Even though it is central to our very existence, it is largely unexplored. It remains mysterious and complex, with interesting, unique, and yet to be discovered relationships between the external world and the internal world. As we begin to look at the various parts of the brain, their interactions with one another, and their relationships with external stimuli, it becomes clear that the study of the brain, including emotion and thought, is still at a point of wonder. Rather than absolute answers there are conjectures, suggestions, and theories. Possibilities open doors to new questions. Such is the way of science!

The neurological study of "Sound-Rage" is akin to setting sail into uncharted waters. The brain processes and then stores information in some locations that are inaccessible to conscious thought or recognition. It creates memories that are locked in particular areas that are immutable. The brain has mechanisms by which different sensory areas overlap. In a unique dance, sounds become associated with visuals, and motion becomes associated with sound.

Indeed, it is as if the syndrome has a life of its own. Even if we eliminated all trigger sounds from the world, the brain would still create triggers that challenge daily living. First, chewing sounds would have to be eliminated before the brain has begun to interpret them as "danger!" If we miss that cut-off, chances are that the sounds have already become neurologically associated with visuals of someone eating or chewing. Once the brain has locked in the association of chewing sounds with the picture of someone eating, the visual itself could well become a trigger. The brain is forming associations with repetition and motion, and soon kicking legs and hair twirling could become triggers. It is just a matter of time before there is a cornucopia of triggers requiring vigilance.

On neurons and the brain
The firing of neurons is what creates emotions, thoughts, movements, perceptions, and the many different components that make up intelligence. There are roughly 86 billion neurons in the brain and over 100 trillion synapses between them. How do these neurons communicate? How is information sent from one brain region to another?

Information is carried by nerve cells by means of patterns of electrical impulses (action potentials or "spikes"). Neurons connect to each other via long, thin protrusions called axons. Once an electrical impulse has reached the end of an axon, the information is transmitted across a synaptic gap to the dendrites of the adjoining neuron. This is accomplished with neurotransmitters, small chemical messengers that convey information from one neuron to the next. Neurotransmitters are released from the axon terminals to cross the synaptic gap and reach the receptor sites of other neurons.

Neural networks are groups of neurons that are synaptically connected to each other. The networks exchange information locally and send information to distant networks throughout the brain. Neural systems, then, are thought to be the basic building blocks of emotions that mediate behavioral interactions with the environment, particularly behaviors that take care of the fundamental problems of survival. When the neural systems are out of whack, behaviors that follow are also out of whack.

Most of the neural connections have plasticity, the ability to change. New connections can be made and reinforced, and established connections can be modified. However, there are parts of the brain that are thought to be "hardwired." Hard-wiring refers to circuitry that is fixed; these are neuronal pathways that cannot be changed by establishing new pathways. The concept of hard-wired or fixed pathways is an important one in the study of "Sound-Rage."

In our study of "Sound-Rage," we are most interested in neural circuits that elicit emotions associated with triggers and the neural processes between emotions and cognitions. We will focus on the auditory, visual, and olfactory sensory systems that provide the input for triggers, and the higher thinking areas of the brain that reinforce the emotions and behaviors.

Quick neural processing
The ability to recognize sounds (to know who/what/where they come from), and to have meaning applied to the sound, relies on complicated neurological processes. There is a complex, albeit fast, journey a sound takes from the first pop of a bubble of chewing gum to the knee jerk feeling of rage. As we think about this journey— how an auditory trigger is evaluated, appraised, reacted to, and stored—we must also note that the process is quick.

The journey begins when sounds are transduced into electrical signals by sensitive hair cell receptors that lie inside the cochlea of the inner ear. The signals are then encoded as volleys of action potentials (defined by Wikipedia as a short-lasting event in which the electrical membrane potential of a cell rapidly rises and falls) by the axons of the vestibulo-cochlear nerve. These are transmitted via a complex chain of nuclei in the brainstem, midbrain, and thalamus of the brain. The auditory signals may take a direct route from the thalamus to the amygdala, or may go from thalamus to the auditory cortex. (These brain regions are discussed in greater detail in the next chapter.)

There is pre-processing in each step of the way. Compared to other sensory systems, in which information reaches the cortex more directly, auditory signals are heavily pre-processed by the time they arrive at the cortex, and this subcortical processing can mediate quite complex auditory tasks.[3]

The brain circuitry is remarkably fast, agile, and fragile. The sequence of events from stimulus to response takes mere seconds even though many processing events are involved.[4] Appraisal (i.e., is the trigger a danger or harmless?) occurs within the first 100 milliseconds (ms) of processing, facilitating rapid responding to survival-relevant cues without the need for conscious, sensory awareness. The sound of smacking lips is heard, travels through the ear to the brain stem, and ultimately to the thalamus and amygdala. In those milliseconds processing is automatic and non-conscious.

The capacity for conscious awareness supported by body arousal and neural feedback, i.e., the evaluation of contextual information requiring controlled processing and activation in the cortex (the higher thinking center of the brain), occurs within seconds. In a relatively brief period of time, the trigger sound has been acknowledged and appraised as "danger!" (and as we will see in later chapters, appraised as pain). Stimulation in the form of firing neurons has sent the lower, more primitive parts of the brain into action. The physical body is now reacting—and the flee response is kicking in. The entire process is now a short term, immediate memory stored in the amygdala.

Over the longer-term scales of minutes to hours, neural plasticity, the ability of the brain to change neural pathways and form new connections, will occur. The cumulative impact of processing, from automatic response to information evaluation in the higher cortices, will influence the way in which neural systems respond to subsequent stimuli, via widespread association networks and arousal modulation.[5]

## How the brain works

Evolutionarily, the fundamental adaptive principle of our brain is to ensure survival. Our most primitive driving motivation is to minimize danger or threat. In psychiatric disorders, there is a breakdown in the ability to focus on relevant information and suppress the irrelevant information.[6] "Sound-Rage" represents an excessive bias towards the signals that express potential danger cues; trigger sounds are interpreted as potential danger cues, yet they are everyday sounds and all day sounds. From the dogs barking first thing in the morning to a neighbor's pounding stereo in the middle of the night, the disorder presents a daily reminder that each and every day presents conflict.

In his book, *The Emotional Brain: the mysterious underpinnings of emotional life*, Joseph LeDoux provides an interesting and compelling discussion on how the brain works. The following concepts provide an overview of topics that are discussed in greater detail in this primer and have both significance and relevance to the syndrome.

One of LeDoux's key premises is that cognition—which comprises rational thought, decision-making, assessment, and evaluation—and emotion are separate but interacting mental functions. And they are mediated by separate but interconnected and interacting brain systems. The emotional brain has its own system. He writes,

> *When a certain region of the brain is damaged, animals or humans lose the capacity to appraise the emotional significance of certain stimuli without any loss in the capacity to perceive the same stimuli as objects. The perceptual representation of an object and the evaluation of the significance of an object are separately processed by the brain.[7]*

In other words, a seemingly innocuous stimulus (sound, visual, or odor) can trigger an automatic, physiological response and feeling (fear, anger, or rage), while at the same time the conscious cognitive brain can think, "Even though I am emotionally exploding, the reality is that someone is simply chewing gum."

*The emotional meaning of a stimulus can begin to be appraised by the brain before the perceptual systems have fully processed the stimulus. It is, indeed, possible for your brain to know that something is good or bad before it knows exactly what it is.*[8]

This refers to the evolutionary advantage of the brain to "know" danger so quickly that you remove your body automatically from the danger before you have the time to process the information. A poisonous snake will strike before you have had time to evaluate the type of snake it is and whether or not it is poisonous. The brain sees the stimulus and you automatically jump back.

As will be discussed later, if the brain is otherwise dysfunctional, it is possible that certain stimuli can be non-consciously perceived as danger even if they are innocuous or harmless. To the dysfunctional brain, a sound can be like a snake, something from which to immediately flee.

*The brain mechanisms through which memories of the emotional significance of stimuli are registered, stored and retrieved are different from the mechanisms through which cognitive memories of the same stimuli are processed.*[9]

Memories are stored in different areas of the brain. Some are retrievable by voluntary processes, whereas others are not. The memories stored in the amygdala are consciously experienced, but they aren't under volitional control. In other words, the memories arise automatically without any effort on your part. While this has an impact on many things, its relevance to the "Sound-Rage" syndrome is apparent.

Memories with emotional content are stored in a critical part of the emotional center of the brain, the amygdala. This is where the dysfunctional brain stores the misinterpreted information about a normally ambiguous or innocuous sound, visual, or odor. The faulty memory mislabels the stimulus as a danger. The misinformation is then retrieved whenever the stimulus occurs, such as when a dog starts barking or when the student sitting next to you starts sniffling, and elicits an emotional and behavioral response.

At the same time, different parts of the brain, such as the hippocampus and cortex, store non-emotional information about the stimuli, such as where the stimuli might appear, who might be creating the trigger, and other external pieces of information associated with the trigger. The conscious thinking part of the brain, the prefrontal cortex, creates thoughts and suppositions about the triggers.

> *The systems that perform emotional appraisals are directly connected with systems involved in the control of emotional responses. Once an appraisal is made by these systems, responses occur automatically. In contrast, systems involved in cognitive processing are not so tightly coupled with response control systems. The hallmark of cognitive processing is flexibility of responses on the basis of processing.* [10]

The irony of this dual system is that while it helps from an evolutionary perspective—you flee the perceived danger—you can not consciously retrieve and "fix" the stored misinformation, so you repeatedly suffer the consequences of harmless signals that are being interpreted as dangerous. At the same time, the thoughts or cognitions about the trigger are retrievable, and, because of this, they take on a relevance and significance that can become problematic. For example, people with "Sound-Rage" will cognitively try to resolve why they are having reactions to triggers, and often conclude that their reaction to the triggers is due to the behaviors of other people. This is discussed in greater detail in Chapters 11 through 15.

# CHAPTER 7
## The Trigger Brain

*Somehow the intricate connectivity of these brain structures gives rise to mental states and accounts for interactions between cognition and emotion that are fundamental to our well-being and our existence.*[1]

*That such signals exist at an early, pre-cortical stage of the auditory pathway only a few synapses removed from sensory transduction in the cochlea highlights the importance of such constructive processes in the brain in interpreting sound. It also is indicative of the many possibilities for sounds to be misinterpreted or miscued.*[2]

<u>Introduction</u>
The brain comprises three layers. The innermost layer, commonly referred to as the "primitive brain," is responsible for instinctive behaviors. The next layer is the limbic system, known for enabling emotions and processing smell (olfaction) and taste (gustation). The third layer is the cerebrum, the "thinking brain," where the processing of detailed sensory information and organizing complex sensory information result in conscious thought.

Emotions originate in a complex network of neuronal nuclei (centers). These centers are situated in a region of the hypothalamus, which is located above the brain stem and below the thalamus, and in a more diffuse region called the limbic system. Within the limbic complex lie several brain parts. These are the amygdala, a region that has been carefully studied with regards to fear, the hippocampus, the insula (or insular cortex), and the pulvinar.

Cortical centers of the cerebrum believed to be involved in the cognitions (thoughts, beliefs, assessments, evaluations etc.) of the "Sound-Rage" disorder are the prefrontal cortex (PFC), the orbitofrontal cortex (OFC), which is a part of the prefrontal cortex, and the anterior cingulate cortex (ACC).

The different brain parts are connected in exceedingly complex ways. The relationships between and among different regions, and the nuances of those relationships, are still not well understood. Information flow among the regions is highly interactive; communication is both feedback and feedforward. (Feedforward communication refers to circuits that carry sensory information from the periphery to the brain stem, thalamus, and then the cortex; feedback refers to circuits that carry information in the other direction.)

<u>Limitations on the science of the brain</u>
When we hear someone eating soup, does the physiological response of fleeing behavior emerge prior to the emotional feeling of anger? Do the emotional feelings arise before, after, or concurrent to the thoughts associated with triggers? Which comes first, an activated range of visceral and behavioral responses or the conscious experience of emotion?

From a neurological perspective, neurons in the emotion-enabling center (amygdala) and the information-processing cortex system often have entangled representations. A single neuron can encode multiple cognitive and emotional variables. This makes separating reactions, thoughts, and feelings exceedingly difficult.[3] And it makes the laboratory study of the relationship between thoughts, emotions, and behavioral responses equally difficult.

The debate about how thought affects emotions and how emotions have an impact on thoughts is ongoing (See Chapter 15 for discussion on cognition.) To circumvent this debate, neuroscientists will often describe cognition and emotion as separable processes, implemented by different regions of the brain. In the study of emotion, scientists measure emotional responses to stimuli along two axes: valence (pleasant versus unpleasant or positive versus negative) and intensity (level of arousal). It is a practical, but limited, way to identify and characterize the neural circuitry responsible for specific aspects of emotional expression and regulation.[4]

In studies with human subjects, neuroscientists sidestep the debate of thought versus emotion by operationally defining a particular aspect of emotion (i.e., defining a particular metric and limiting the study to the evaluation of that specific metric); they then use a specific behavioral or physiological characterization to investigate the neural basis of the emotional process. For example, to investigate anger, neuroscientists first operationally define anger. Then they create a very specific situation from which they hope to stimulate or elicit anger, such as showing angry faces or sticking a pin in subjects' fingers. They look at the subjects' brains and record the areas that are firing.

Researchers create simulations of events to elicit basic emotions, since it is virtually impossible to simulate the authentic emotional responses that are generated in real-world situations. These artificial simulations are often accompanied by a small sample size. The validity and legitimacy in generalizing outcomes to an overall population is questionable, particularly in light of the limitations of the research conditions, not the least of which is inadequately creating a genuine emotional response.

The trigger brain parts
We have only a preliminary understanding of the nature of the processing of sound signals from the brain stem to upper cortical areas. Processing and transformation take place at many stops along the route from someone sniffing to a sufferer storming out of the room. Which brain parts interpret the sound? At what juncture does a sound go from ambiguous to "danger!" Is it possible that danger may actually be interpreted as pain?

The ear
The ear and hearing anomalies are not implicated in this disorder. There is no evidence that there is a relationship between hearing disorders such as hyperacusis or tinnitus and "Misophonia." Nevertheless, audiologists can play a role in treatment of the disorder. Relief is often found in the form of white noise generators attached to the ear. (See the discussion of therapy in Chapter 17.) From the ear, encoded sound travels through the brain stem and the inferior colliculus of the midbrain and is processed at each brain region.

## The brain stem and inferior colliculus

The inferior colliculus (IC) is a necessary relay for nearly all ascending and descending auditory information situated mid-way along the auditory pathways of the midbrain. A relevant point regarding the inferior colliculus associated with "Sound-Rage" is its role in distinguishing environmental from self-generated sounds.[5, See note 1] This may account for why people with "Sound-Rage" are not bothered by the sounds of their own chewing.

## Periaqueductal Gray

Periaqueductal Gray (PAG, also called the "central gray") is the cell-dense region surrounding the midbrain aqueduct. It commands primitive fight or flight reactions elicited by threat, acute pain, or asphyxia,[6] and has a role in the fleeing response. The PAG provides input to the IC and may therefore provide limbic information to the auditory system.

## Thalamus

The thalamus relays incoming sensory pathways to appropriate areas of the cortex. The auditory thalamus is the major source of auditory projections which ultimately reach the lateral nucleus (LA) of the amygdala. The medial geniculate body (MGB) is the main auditory center of the thalamus; it gets input from the inferior colliculus and provides output to the auditory cortex as well as the amygdala. The MGB also gets input from the thalamic reticular nucleus (TRN) which forms a thin veil around the dorsal thalamus and acts as a filter, sieving information between thalamus and cortex. The TRN allows signals to pass to the cortex or blocks them by innervating and inhibiting thalamic projection neurons.[7]

## Pulvinar

The pulvinar complex is the largest nuclear mass in the thalamus. It receives direct visual input from the retina, indirect visual input via the superficial layers of the superior colliculus in the mid-brain, and massive input from visual cortices.[8] Connections between brain regions that have a role in evaluation of a stimulus, the pulvinar, amygdala, orbitofrontal cortex, and the insula, suggest that the pulvinar may have a role in emotion processing.[9, See note 2]

Amygdala

The amygdala is a structurally heterogeneous collection of nuclei, lying in the anterior medial portion of each temporal lobe. Neurons in the lateral amygdala (LA) and basal nuclei (BA) have large dendritic trees. Extensive connections within and between the different nuclei of the amygdaloidal complex add to the complexity of the brain region, making it difficult for us to annotate precise connections and mechanisms of how stimuli are perceived and how memories are formed.

Perhaps more than any other brain region, the amygdala has been implicated in numerous neuropsychiatric and neurodevelopmental disorders. It is considered the integrative center for emotions, emotional behavior, and motivation. Convergent information from all sensory modalities originating in high-order visual, auditory, olfactory, gustatory, visceral, somatosensory, and polymodal cortices reaches the amygdala, as does information from the viscera or the internal parts of the body.

Overall, the amygdala is an intricately connected brain region that interacts and affects emotional responses. It receives information from temporal and insular cortices, the auditory cortex, the visual cortex and regions of the prefrontal cortex. And it sends out information to many regions, including the hippocampus (memory), the prefrontal cortex, and the sensory cortices.[10]

The amygdala plays a role in signaling valence (pleasant/positive or unpleasant/negative affect) of the sensory stimuli that it receives. In other words, the amygdala assigns some meaning to the incoming stimuli.[11] The amygdala, as well as a network of cortical and subcortical areas, activates during exposure to aversive sounds.[12] The amygdala also activates during exposure to aversive visual, olfactory, and gustatory stimuli.[See note 3]

External auditory stimuli reach the amygdala via two different pathways which complement each other. A short route comes from the thalamus; it is relatively fast, allowing the body to prepare for potential danger before knowing exactly what the danger is. As well, sensory information is transmitted to the amygdala through neural cascades that originate in the primary sensory cortices such as the auditory cortex. The amygdala is therefore poised to integrate both fast, automatic responses with slower, more cognitive responses.

In turn, the amygdala will send signals to regions of the brain involved in autonomic control if the incoming information from the periphery presents "danger." Output from the amygdala quickly activates other limbic areas, causing the person to react immediately.[13] The behavioral responses are generated primarily through the central and medial nuclei of the amygdala which project to hypothalamic and brainstem centers involved in autonomic control.

### The amygdala and "Sound-Rage"

In most psychiatric disorders, the dysfunctional brain creates strategies for coping with stimuli that are perceived as threat. In these disorders, including the full range of phobias, panic disorder, and PTSD, fear is the underlying driver of the strategy. The amygdala has been implicated as the key brain part for processing fear, reacting to threatening stimuli through fear, and storing learned memories about fear-inducing situations and environments.

In fear schemes, stimuli may go directly to the amygdala; the body responds without thinking, such as jumping back when coming upon a snake. It is fear that initiates the immediate flight paradigm. However, there are no data to indicate that the amygdala is the center of anger. As well, there is no scientific evidence to support that the amygdala is the first port-of-call in a "Sound-Rage" trigger's path from brain stimuli to flight behavior. *A neurological flight paradigm in response to anger characterized by the "Sound-Rage" disorder has never been studied.*

### Amygdala and sensory sensitivity

There is evidence that once the amygdala is sensitized to a traumatic event or trigger, there is a change in the way the sensory input is processed. Previous emotionally salient events have been stored in the memory of the amygdala where they are non-conscious, implicit, and irretrievable. A similar stimulus or one of lesser intensity may trigger a memory and result in the same fast response that the original trigger elicited. If a sensory stimulus was previously associated with a traumatic event, the person will respond to similar stimuli with the same emotional response, even though the stimuli are harmless.

This is best illustrated by emotional processing of visual stimuli in posttraumatic stress disorder (PTSD). A functional magnetic resonance imaging (fMRI) study exploring the processing of trauma-related pictures in the visual cortex and amygdala of twenty combat veterans found that the amygdala had increased activation, irrespective of the content of the pictures, and regardless of the recognition intensity of the images.

The emotional trauma changed the amygdala's threshold for response in such a way that intensity did not matter. The results suggest that, at least in PTSD veterans, emotional traumatic experience can modify visual processing at the pre-attentive level. It might point to a possible predisposed mechanism for pathological processing of traumatic experience. In either case, both suggestions point to the amygdala as becoming sensitized and reacting to visual stimuli from previous trauma or a predisposition.[14] How does this relate to "Sound-Rage"? It infers that *the amygdala, with its vast connectivity to higher thinking centers and the flight response centers, may be predisposed or sensitized in such a way as to change its threshold for arousal.*

Amygdala and memory
Deciphering the emotional significance of sensory stimuli enables emotional memory formation. The amygdala may play a role in stimulating memory formation beyond its part in sending neuromodulatory signals to other brain regions. Brain imaging studies have found a correlation between amygdala activation during encoding and subsequent memory. The correlation would look like this: amygdala activation reflects moment-to-moment subjective emotional experience. This activation enhances memory in relation to the emotional intensity of an experience. Therefore, a repeated emotional experience will be encoded and put into memory.

What does this mean with regards to "Sound-Rage"? The repeated emotional intensity of hearing chewing sounds, dogs barking, legs swinging etc. is activating and re-activating the amygdala and enhancing memory storage.[15] The memories stored in the amygdala are non-conscious, indelible, and non-retrievable. *It might be that these stored, unconscious memories make it increasingly difficult to "move on" from the disorder.*

In an experiment of induced stress versus a control group, researchers found that exposure to aversive stimuli caused a prolonged activation of both the amygdala and its connections with parts of the brain involved in the stress response. This might cause associated stimuli to become more salient (important, or to stand out).[16] With regards to "Sound-Rage," repeated experiences are helping to form the memory, reinforcing whatever initial dysfunction there may be. With the memories of stress being laid down, information sent to the cortex is emphatic: "danger!"

Auditory cortex
The auditory cortex's functional organization resembles the organization of the cortices devoted to other sensory modalities. Ascending information comes via the thalamus, which in turn projects to 'higher-level' cortical areas. The neurons in auditory cortex interpret incoming sound signals and send them to the rest of the nervous system.

Many neurons in the auditory cortex respond only to very specific sounds. According to one study, only 5% of neurons in the auditory cortex had a "high firing rate" when receiving a range of sounds of varying length, frequency, and volume. The researchers hypothesized that each neuron in the auditory cortex may have an "optimal stimulus" to which it is particularly sensitized.[17] Studies have suggested that it is possible that sounds, such as the clicking of fingernails on a computer laptop or the clicking sound of high heels on pavement, might be processed and have assigned meaning at the auditory cortex level.[18]

Prefrontal cortex
The cerebrum is the largest part of the human brain, containing all of the centers that receive and interpret sensory information. The prefrontal cortex (PFC) located in the anterior portion of the cerebral

cortex is made up of a group of brain areas with extensive interconnections between different PFC sub-regions. This allows information to be shared within local networks, as well as to converge with sensory cortices in multiple modalities.[19]

The PFC has a role in the cognitive and emotional interpretation of valenced sensory stimuli and in controlling subsequent behavioral responses. Studies suggest that both the functional and the electrophysiological characteristics of the amygdala and the PFC overlap and intimately depend on each other. *The neural circuits mediating cognitive (thought), emotional (mood, feelings, affect), physiological (body), and behavioral (action) responses appear to be inextricably linked and may not truly be separable.*[20]

Orbitofrontal cortex

The orbitofrontal cortex (OFC) is a prefrontal cortex region located in the frontal lobes that plays a critical role in emotional appraisal and social cognition. It receives rich multimodal information from all sensory association cortices, and may provide an additional route through which sensory information reaches the amygdala. Based on anatomical and functional data, it has been proposed that it is a convergence region that might promote the integration of multimodal sensory information with affective reactions. It might be involved in aspects of affective appraisal, subsequent to automatic stages of processing taking place in the amygdala and sensory cortices, by integrating initial evaluations with other cognitive factors related to context, goals, or task demands.[21]

Brain imaging data have shown that the OFC is involved in the processing of non-vocal auditory emotional events, emotional prosody (an individual's tone of voice, conveyed through changes in pitch, loudness, timbre, speech rate, and pauses), and music perception. A recent study with human subjects investigated changes in cerebral blood flow with positron emission tomography during exposure to unpleasant auditory stimuli. They found that the caudal orbitofrontal cortex responds in the face of unpleasant incoming auditory information.[22]

Insula

The insula (or insular cortex) is the hub of a cortical network of regions, and provides an interface of feelings, cognition, and action through its integration of visual, tactile, and auditory information. It has been implicated in processing recall-generated sadness, anger, fear, disgust, happiness, and aversive emotional stimuli. The posterior insular cortex is functionally connected to sensory areas.

The insular cortex has bidirectional connections to the amygdala and the orbitofrontal cortex, and is thus centrally placed to receive information about the salience (the importance of) and relative value (pleasantness/positive or unpleasantness/negative) of the stimulus environment. [See notes 4 and 5] The insula focuses on how the value of stimuli might affect the state of the body. Functional neuroimaging studies have linked insular cortex activation to perceptual awareness of threat, coding of pain intensity, and expectation of painful stimuli, all aspects of the "Sound-Rage" disorder. Painful stimuli activate the insular cortex, and anticipation of emotionally aversive stimuli activates the right insular cortex. The insula is implicated in empathy and compassion, which are critical to effective therapy (discussed in Chapter 17). Empathy is also a component of mimicry, a behavior relevant to "Sound-Rage." (See Chapter 12 for a detailed discussion.)

The Anterior cingulate cortex
The anterior cingulate cortex (ACC) is connected with the prefrontal cortex and processes top-down and bottom-up stimuli. It has close and heavy projections into brain regions typically involved in affective, motivational, and autonomic processing— the amygdala, hypothalamus, and anterior insula—and is involved in assessing the salience of emotion and motivational information. This connectivity suggests that the ACC has a role in the generation of emotion-related physiological reactions and behavioral responses[23] as well as autonomic responses to emotionally salient stimuli. It is believed to be crucial in the production of subjective feelings, executive functioning, and coordinating appropriate responses to internal and external events. *The ACC is also a key region for assessing the affect of pain.*

# CHAPTER 8
Brain Circuitry and Triggers

*There are two "roads" for auditory stimuli to reach the amygdala from the thalamus for emotional response: one to the auditory cortex, which in turn has connections to the amygdale, and one directly to the amygdale central nucleus. The advantage of having two roads is that the direct route saves time.*

*In danger and stress situations, the time saved is literally a matter of life or death. It is possible that the direct pathway is responsible for the control of emotional responses that we don't understand. This may occur in all of us some of the time, but may be a predominant mode of functioning in individuals with certain emotional disorders.[1]*

## Introduction

We solve the mysteries of the relationships between triggers, perceived threat, and rage by studying the brain. The circuitry within the human brain is complex, confusing, and poorly understood,[See note 1] with inextricable links between thoughts and feelings.[2] Added to the challenge of interconnectedness is the fact that changes occur within the brain throughout one's lifetime: pathways break, some because of developmental changes in the brain. New pathways form, while a certain number of pathways remain fixed. (Fixed pathways are often referred to as "hard-wired," and the behaviors that come from these pathways as "innate.")

Trillions of inter-connections are made even more complex by the remarkably quick firing of signals. It might be a matter of milliseconds (ms) that separates one area activating before another, and mere seconds that pass before the brain has evaluated and stored information. No wonder it is difficult to ascertain where and how a particular trigger gained its significance as a danger.

## "Sound-Rage" circuitry introduction

One of the most in-depth studies of audition, emotion, and the brain circuitry comes from the work of LeDoux. (For more on LeDoux, refer to Chapter 6.) However, the circuitry that he studies concentrates on fear. The "Misophonia" or "Sound-Rage" disorder has a different circuitry, one that connects anger, pain perception, and the creation, maintenance, and generalization of response to triggers.

Acoustic signals in the environment are picked up by special receptors in the ear. They are transmitted into the brain by way of the auditory nerve, which terminates in the auditory brainstem nuclei. Axons from these regions mostly cross over to the other side of the brain and ascend to the inferior colliculus of the midbrain. From the inferior colliculus, axons travel to the auditory thalamic relay nucleus. At the thalamus, an auditory stimulus goes one of two routes. Neurons in the auditory area of the thalamus project directly to auditory cortex, or auditory information in the form of activated firing neurons travel the shorter, faster sub-cortical route from the thalamus directly to the lateral amygdala (LA).

The journey of a trigger stimulus from the amygdala or auditory cortex might look like this: Within a few dozens of milliseconds, information travels from both the amygdala and the auditory cortex to other areas of cortex where the stimulus is further processed and evaluated. Information travels through a circuit to the insular cortex, a brain region that co-mingles evaluations of threat, pain, and anger.

The insular cortex will send its interpretation of the stimulus back down in the brain in a process called feedback; it will feed information back to the amygdala (or through other neural circuits to brain stem areas) to motivate and drive the body to a behavioral response away from the danger.[See note 2] This interconnectedness will be demonstrated to have significance to "Sound-Rage" in the study of pain. (See Chapter 12 for greater detail.)

A trigger's phenomenological details, such as who is chewing or what their mouth looks like, and the brain's response of "this is a threat!" may travel as a feedforward pathway via yet another circuit.

Emotionally intense experiences and undue stress activate the amygdala, and evidence indicates that the activation is correlated to encoding and memory in the amygdala. The feedforward information, such as a significant other's chewing sounds, may go to the hippocampus or amygdala for storage. The memory of the original stimuli (trigger) or the response to the original stimuli (rage) is stored. Once there, it is now an implicit memory.

*The amygdala (and perhaps other brain regions) stores an association that is irretrievable to the conscious mind. That association may be a blend of the stimulus, like a chewing sound; the phenomenological details, such as who is chewing; the brain's interpretation of the stimuli's salience or importance; and the affect of rage and anger.*

### From the thalamus to the amygdala

The thalamus-to-amygdala-to-flight behavior is the least complex brain circuitry theory in the "Sound-Rage" disorder. Cells in the thalamic areas that project to the amygdala respond to a wide range of stimuli from different sensory modalities, such as sound and sight. The information from the thalamus that goes directly to the amygdala is not modulated (adjusted or regulated) by the cortex. The stimuli are unfiltered and biased toward evoking responses, and to this end, the circuitry has been described as "coarse."

For example, stimuli that are known to connote visual or auditory threats, like staring eyes or threatening vocalization, are conveyed directly to the lateral nucleus of the amygdala (LA). Here, within the amygdala, the original value of a stimulus is indelibly coded.[3] The LA, in turn, connects with the central amygdala (CE). The CE connects with the hypothalamus and the brain stem,[See note 3] putting the flight response in motion.

> *Scenario 1: At the breakfast table, the family sits down to eat morning cereal, drink orange juice, and sip on coffee. All of a sudden, Lyndon, a nine year old boy, hears the chewing sounds his mother is making. Unbeknownst to him, there has been a fundamental change in his brain. The sound travels quickly from*

*the ear, through the auditory passageway, to the thalamus. Something triggers a reaction that signifies a threat or extremely potent danger. Within milliseconds, the danger warning is communicated through the firing of neurons that go from the lateral amygdala to the central amygdala, and on to the lower brain stem regions that work to get the body moving away from danger.*

## Amygdala to the auditory cortex circuitry

The amygdala provides information to the auditory cortex. Certain sounds, such as the scraping of chalk or finger nails on a blackboard, are known by all of us as very unpleasant. Those sounds enhance activation of the auditory cortex, relative to neutral sounds. Using modeling techniques, it was demonstrated that connections from the amygdala to the auditory cortex are modulated by perceived unpleasantness (valence). [4, See note 4]

## Auditory cortex circuitry

However, information from the thalamus can take a cortical route to the primary sensory cortex, the auditory cortex. Here, the auditory cortex can confirm the threat or determine that danger is not present. This circuit is more complex and neurotransmitters play a critical role at each stage of travel. [5]

The auditory cortex provides information to "higher" cortical regions [See note 5] that ascribe meaning to the stimulus. (It has been suggested that the amygdala seeks information from higher thinking centers of the brain to help resolve uncertainty in the environment. [6, See note 6]) The cortex may ascertain that the stimulus is "danger!" or "pain." The assessment goes back to the emotional centers that can ascribe fleeing behaviors, i.e., it is fed back to the amygdala and the thalamus.

This relationship has significance in the "Sound-Rage" disorder. Information from the auditory cortex to the amygdala might lead to an enhanced representation of trigger stimuli that are frequently encountered or of particular significance, such as the auditory-trigger sound of gum popping. [7] In fact, given the brain's interconnectivity, the impact of the amygdala on behavior can be mediated through many routes, such as via the visual cortex, the auditory cortex, or the prefrontal cortex.[8]

Orbitofrontal cortex circuitry
The amygdala projects to the thalamus, which robustly projects to the orbitofrontal cortex. In turn, the OFC has robust connections to and from cortical representations of smell, sight, and sound. Intrinsic connections link prefrontal areas, enabling the synthesis of sensory information and emotional context that are necessary for selective attention and action, which are processes considered crucial for learning and memory.[See note 7] This particular circuit has been implicated in the pathology of disorders such as obsessive-compulsive disorder (OCD), autism spectrum disorder, and attention-deficit/hyperactivity disorder (ADHD).[9]

The amygdala and insular cortex circuitry
Some amygdalar sites that are connected with the OFC are also connected with insular sensory cortices that are involved in the regulation of physiological changes related to emotional states[10] and are associated with emotional significance.[11, See note 8] In particular, the insular region is known for anger and for evaluating the intensity of the unpleasantness of pain.

The insula may play a significant role in psychopathology, and in specific, may play a key role in "Sound-Rage." Most recent research attention in anxiety disorders has focused on a key role of amygdala abnormalities; there are several reasons to consider the notion that pathological anxiety is etiologically (causally) related to insula function instead of (or in addition to) altered amygdala function.[12]

*The insula is also implicated in Tourette syndrome and may offer a clue as to the developmental onset of "Sound-Rage."*

From the cortex to sub-cortical regions
Regions like the insular cortex, anterior cingulate cortex, and the orbitofrontal cortex, modulate subcortical target regions, like the amygdala, by a complex set of cascading projections. These cascades excite / activate or subdue / suppress subcortical activity.

These multiple descending pathways, from cortical areas to subcortical autonomic regions in the hypothalamus, PAG, and brainstem, produce a complex pattern of autonomic regulation.[See note 9]

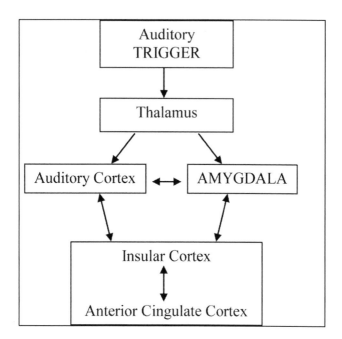

*Scenario 2: The sound of sipping coffee is sent from the thalamus to the primary sensory auditory cortex. From here, it is sent to other cortical regions, such as the insular cortex. At the insular cortex, the sound is perceived as "danger" and perhaps the unpleasantness (not the sensation) of pain. In seconds, the input is evaluated as salient. The emotion of anger/rage in reaction to pain is stimulated in the insular cortex. Connection to the ventral part of the anterior cingulate cortex assesses the salience of emotion and motivational information. This information is connected with amygdala nucleus accumbens and hypothalamus and a flight response is activated. Information fed back to the amygdala also feeds the insular cortex, the emotional center for anger. The original stimulus is stored in memory. All of this occurs within seconds.*

## Anterior cingulate cortex (ACC) and insular cortex relationship

Both anterior cingulate cortex and insular cortex are core regions of a salience network responsive to a wide range of stimuli relevant to emotional and /or motivational states. The insula integrates sensory information into awareness, and this information is then transferred to the ACC. Conjointly, they process salience and attentional direction. Co-activation of the anterior insular cortex (AIC) and ACC is reported by numerous functional neuroimaging studies of emotional processing.

AIC and ACC are amongst a network of regions activated by a task eliciting empathy for the pain of others, and thus may be crucial for empathy. Given the mass of evidence that AIC and ACC are both implicated in emotional processing and first-person subjective experience, it is reasonable to suppose that functional abnormalities of these regions may be involved in the pathophysiology of psychiatric disorders.[13] *It is likely that these two regions of higher processing are intimately tied to the "Sound-Rage" disorder through mediation of attention to external stimuli, processing stimuli salience, and connectivity with emotional centers.*

## Visual stimuli processing

For the vast majority of sufferers, the first and primary triggers are chewing sounds. However, the repertoire of auditory triggers expands (see Chapter 16 for a detailed discussion) to include visual triggers. Like auditory stimuli, visual stimuli that have affective and motivational significance can engage multiple brain sites—including the amygdala, OFC, anterior insula cortex (AIC) and anterior cingulate cortex (ACC). These brain sites are also known centers for anger and perception of pain and, as we will see later, are implicated in the "Sound-Rage" disorder.

Most brain imaging studies on the effects of interaction between emotion and attention have concerned the visual domain, although these primarily focus on the study of fear and the processing of facial emotions. However, recent brain imaging data show that the emotional value of visual stimuli can strongly influence neuronal responsiveness in other sensory and memory systems,[14] implying that the reactions to visual triggers get stored in memory, and the response to the visual stimuli can affect or be affected by other sensory systems.

After traveling through cells in the retina, visual information is further processed sub-cortically in both the pulvinar and the lateral geniculate nucleus the thalamus. The pulivar[See note 10] receives input directly from the retina, as well as highly processed visual input from the superior colliculus and the visual cortex areas. This portion of the thalamus is believed to have the potential to integrate information from very diverse brain regions.

As in audition, the amygdala is implicated in the emotional processing of visual stimuli. The amygdala participates in the recognition of visual emotional signals from two mechanisms: a subcortical route (via superior colliculus and the pulvinar thalamus) and a longer, cortical route via the visual neocortex.[15] Lateral and basal nuclei of the amygdala receive input from visual cortex and sensory association cortex. This information is combined with inputs from other sensory modalities. This may be one way that the brain associates visual and auditory stimuli.

Once a visual stimulus is associated with an auditory trigger, such as the sight of a person chewing gum from a distance, the stimulus has acquired relevance or salience. The visual stimulus can become a trigger and will activate /excite the pulvinar thalamus. Whereas earlier, someone pointing their finger or kicking their legs would be an ambiguous or neutral visual image, it now has taken on significance.[See note 11]

Olfaction and the brain
The sensation of smell as a trigger in "Sound-Rage" appears to come into being after auditory and visual triggers have been established. The reaction to an aversive smell is typically disgust, and may be associated with other triggers through this particular reaction. This does not imply that a trigger sound is associated with odor; there are few, if any, stories or testimonies that equate smell with rage. However, there is a relationship between triggers and disgust. Even though we often perceive odors while hearing auditory stimuli, surprisingly little is known about auditory–olfactory integration.

The sensation of smell is an evolutionary tool for survival. It helps humans find food and to avoid the places where predators live and lurk. The sense of olfaction is often reported to have a special relationship with emotional processing, evoking memories as well as emotional responses. In fact, people can identify a smell with happiness, disgust, and anxiety.[16]

In this wide expanse of function, olfaction is integrated into all aspects of sensation and is incorporated into many of our reactions to stimuli. Olfactory sensory neurons project axons to the brain within the olfactory nerve. These nerve fibers pass to the olfactory bulb through perforations in the cribriform plate, which in turn projects olfactory information to the olfactory cortex.[17] The olfactory piriform cortex is continuous with the anterior portion of the amygdala and projects directly to the amygdala and posterior OFC. It is also connected to the insular cortex. This anatomy suggests a high level of functional connectivity between the olfactory emotion-systems and the insular cortex, a center that assesses both danger and pain.

Aversive odors activate the amygdala[18] and neurologic studies have found functional connectivity between the olfactory cortex, the amygdala, and hippocampus in response to negative odor.[19] There is demonstrated modulation of signal in the anterior insula during trials combining negatively valenced odor and disgusted faces.[20] The insular cortex is activated by a broad range of disgust-related stimuli. Since the insula is involved in conscious perception of emotional bodily feelings in general, disgust contributes to our decision-making with regards to approach versus avoidance.[21] Unpleasant odors initiate disgust and perhaps disgust is associated with a trigger.

Brain circuitry and lack of awareness
Sometimes it seems as if the sound trigger appears out of nowhere. For example, you are sitting on a bus reading a magazine and you become aware of the gum popping of a gum chewer. Almost instinctively, your body becomes agitated. How did the brain process what was barely acknowledged? Imagine that you are afraid of cats.

Picture that you walk into a room and there is a cat sleeping under the table. Your eyes scan the room, and even though you do not consciously notice that there is a cat on the floor, your brain is alerted. You have an immediate physiological response even if you can not consciously say why.

One possible explanation is that once sensitized, the brain stores information and reacts on its own, that is, subcortical circuits may elicit reactions even when stimuli are not consciously perceived.

Brain activation prior to explicit awareness of an emotionally salient social stimulus was studied with functional magnetic resonance imagery (fMRI). Using visual representation of faces and houses as stimuli, researchers ascertained neural activation in the amygdala, pulvinar, insular, and early visual cortex, even when the visual stimuli were suppressed from view. The researchers suggested that awareness is not necessary for information to reach the higher order cognitive-cortical areas regarding emotionally charged objects.[22]

# CHAPTER 9
## The Brain and Multi-Sensory Processing

*Our views are rapidly changing about the stimulus-specificity of cortical areas that have long been viewed as belonging exclusively to one or other of the senses.*[1]

The type and number of rage-inducing triggers expand through time. While the number of triggers within the sensory modality of sound increases, so does the likelihood that new triggers will develop from another sensory modality, vision. Neurologically, triggers expand through a mechanism called multisensory processing. Sensory areas of the brain are highly interconnected, and inputs from different modalities (such as audition and vision) can affect each other's processing. Advances in brain imaging have clearly demonstrated that unisensory inputs do not get processed in isolation; the old paradigm of a sensory region recognizing only one specific type of input is changing.

The brain comprises many interactive neural pathways that overlap. It is not just the amygdala that processes the sounds as "danger!" and it is not just sounds that represent threat. The brain's capability to have several different sensory inputs merge at an early stage of processing presents new possibilities for how information is non-consciously interpreted. There is growing evidence that activity in the auditory cortex, which is a relatively "early" cortex processing region, can be heavily influenced by inputs other than those arising directly from the auditory thalamus. Similarly, activity in visual cortex can be modulated by non-visual stimuli.

There has been a long-standing view that the meeting or overlap of multi-sensory information occurs in higher-order association areas of the neocortex, although this view has changed with the advent of advanced neuroimaging technology. In the traditional paradigm, neurobiologists assume that multisensory integration is a higher order process that occurs after sensory signals have undergone extensive processing through a hierarchy of unisensory subcortical and cortical regions. Multi-sensory integration of sounds and sights and smells are thought to happen after stimuli are processed through their separate cortices, the auditory cortex, the visual cortex, or the olfactory center. Lower unisensory centers process rudimentary information, such as the detection of simple stimulus features, while the higher processes put together the pieces of sight, sound, smell, taste, and how the body feels into conscious percepts. In this schema of how the brain works, the convergence of information is deferred until after the unisensory cortices have done their job.

However, neuroimaging studies in humans, nonhuman primates, and other species are now showing that multisensory convergence happens in low level cortical structures or earlier structures in the brain, implying earlier-in-time processing.[2] This was demonstrated in a 2003 study that investigated the nature of somatosensory (skin, skeleton, and internal organs) input to the caudomedial (CM) region of the macaque monkey's auditory cortex. The study presented physiological evidence of multisensory convergence at an early stage of cortical auditory processing in monkeys, suggesting that inputs from different modalities converge at very early stages of cortical sensory processing.[3]

We have envisioned the sound of someone smacking his/her lips as coming up through the brain stem, the mid brain, landing in the thalamus, and traveling on independently to either the amygdala or the auditory cortex. But the brain is more complex and nuanced. Multisensory interactions can occur shortly after response onset, at the lowest cortical processing stages.

Visual stimuli and olfaction overlap, and provide more data from which the brain can assess threat or associate with threat. Auditory inputs have been found to modulate processing in regions of the lateral occipital (visual) cortices. The combined influence of visual and auditory inputs on object identification starts early in the processing of information. The convergence of sight information, sound information, and internal organ/skin response information in the auditory cortex implies an environment rich in detail, with the auditory stimuli being the predominant subject of processing. The fact that auditory input merges with visual information processing at a very early stage has interesting implications for how early processing of a trigger can impact the processing of other stimuli.[4,] See note 1

Information from the primary sensory cortices makes its way via neural pathways to the anterior cingulate cortex (ACC). The ACC, which is closely united with the insular cortex and the frontal cortices, is more active in response to visual stimuli associated with multisensory information than stimuli with a unisensory past. Even when an object is easily identifiable through a single sensory modality, input from other sensory modalities facilitates object recognition. Seeing a person take a spoon to a bowl may be as compelling to the brain as the subsequent clicking sound that it makes.[5]

An interesting question is, "how are non-auditory inputs contributing to the brain's assessment of a sound?" A "Misophonia" sufferer can readily attest that seeing a person chewing gum quickens the response time of a rage reaction, even though the auditory component (the sound of gum chewing) is enough to create a response. In fact, just the sight of the person chewing can elicit a response.

One possibility for cross-modality of sound to vision, such as the common visual trigger of seeing a person eat, rather than hearing someone eat, comes from the "McGurk Effect" observation of how we learn and process speech. Speech information comes from hearing and processing words and visual cues like the movements of the teeth, tongue, mouth, and non-mouth facial features. According to the McGurk Effect, the visual information ascertained from seeing a person speak changes the way we hear the sound; once the senses are integrated, it is not possible to separate them. The physical movements of speech, mouth, and lips create the acoustic and visual signals.[6]

Non-auditory inputs contribute to the brain's assessment of a sound by providing characteristic environmental information relevant to the sound. Somatosensory and visual inputs have greater spatial precision than simple hearing input. Think of the number of times you have heard a sound but could not identify its location. Birds singing from a tree—but which tree? You turn your head and consciously look for the sound's point of origin. Or you are in a busy market with your young children, and from behind you hear a young child calling "mommy." If you saw that your children were in front of you, most likely you wouldn't react. However, if you weren't sure where all your children were, you would instinctively turn around to see if the cry for help came from one of your offspring. This response is an automatic, non-conscious response; you would turn around without even thinking about it. The precision of visual input and the information you get from skin or skeleton ("I feel it in my bones") might support auditory spatial localization.

What does this accomplish? This additional input might influence the perceptual salience or relative importance of a particular sound. While the subjective experience would remain predominantly auditory, it may take on associated meaning through the integration of visual and somatosensory information.

# CHAPTER 10
A Developmental Disorder: What Can Sudden Onset Tell Us?

*There is a profound lack of information on circuit formation, cell fate during development and neurochemical compensation in either humans or the animals used to model neurodegenerative diseases.*[1]

*In the not too distant future, it might be worth considering having the community of misophonics have their genomes sequenced... If a genetic basis could be identified it would greatly increase our ability to understand and eventually perhaps treat the disorder. Currently all such genomic studies are, to my knowledge, initiated by medical researchers. But as the price of genomic sequencing plummets, it will make sense for people with "orphan" diseases to compile such data sets themselves. Once the data are collected, it probably wouldn't be difficult to find researchers with the skill and interest in analyzing them for any possible causal mutation. It would potentially be a whole new way of doing this kind of science.*[2]

*There might be an innate disfunction (sp) with the plasticity in certain brain circuits. Plasticity in all the brains systems is an innately determined characteristic. An innate capacity for synapses to record and store information is what allows systems to encode experiences. If the synapse of a particular brain system cannot change, this system will not have the ability to be modified by experience. Thus, it is possible that the connection between the initial trigger and the initial reaction of fear is due to a damaged synapse (whatever or wherever that may be), and this damage may also be unmodifiable.*[3]

*It started suddenly when I was 8 or 9 years old*[4]

Introduction

Neurological disorders are pathological conditions that impair the proper functioning of the brain, often by disrupting sensory and/or motor networks. Developmental neurological disorders are caused by genetic and/or environmental factors that adversely affect the nervous system during development. The onset can be sudden, and can become apparent during childhood.

"Sound-Rage" appears to be a developmental neurological disorder that manifests suddenly and primarily in childhood. Many sufferers share a similar story, a recollection that the trigger reactions simply started, implying that there was a period of years in early childhood when the sufferer was symptom-free. Many of the first explicit memories of onset identify a specific auditory trigger, most likely a chewing-related stimulus, and a specific source, predominantly a parent but occasionally a sibling. What remains strong is the explicit memory of the emotion it generated (anger) and the subsequent response (escaping).

The transformation of the developing brain presents a provocative landscape for the onset of the disorder. The "Sound-Rage" brain's development trajectory differs from the norm. After spending six, or eleven, or thirteen years of being unaffected by and barely acknowledging ambient sounds of breathing, chewing, taping, clicking etc., the brain suddenly becomes attentive to certain sounds.

A once-ambiguous phenomenon—a sound that blends into the environment—becomes a focal point for attention and observation. The sound (or in some cases, the visual trigger) becomes assessed as salient or standing out. Its signal is processed as negatively valenced or highly unpleasant, and a threat to survival. The signal is one of danger and, as suggested in this primer, the cause of affective, non-sensation pain.

Based on sufferer's biographies and testimonies (stories), the estimated range of age-of-onset tends to be between the ages of 8 and 13, or late childhood through mid-adolescence. There have been accounts of age of onset in earlier childhood and in the early teen years and several reports, although significantly fewer, of an adult onset (age 18 or greater). Having a discrete age of onset range signifies that there is a developmental component to the disorder. Given the prevalence of the age of onset prior to puberty, the disorder could be considered a developmental childhood disorder.

Being a developmental disorder presents fundamental questions. What are the mechanisms that shift in such a way so that non-threatening or ambiguous stimuli acquire a threat value? Is it a chemical change having an impact on a neurotransmitter, creating new firings or new inhibitions? Is it a physical breakdown in cortical matter? Is it a breakdown of the normal pathways for electrical impulses to be carried from one neuron to another? What part of the brain is affected?

Many of the vulnerabilities of the brain might depend on the first two decades of life.[5] In the first two decades, gray matter thickness, density, and cortical shape change. With about 100 billion neurons at birth, the human brain follows a developmental course of growth and pruning with significant pruning occurring during adolescence. Dendritic branching of neurons and the numbers of synaptic connections greatly decrease. Conduction speed of fibers that interconnect different brain regions increases as layers of insulating lipids are laid down on axons through the process of myelination.[6] Concurrently, large scale connections from prefrontal cortex to the rest of the brain remain incomplete.

Developmental changes
Gray-matter volumes generally decline after age 7, perhaps because the advancement of white matter throughout childhood begins to overtake the overall rate of brain volume expansion. The decrease in frontal grey matter volume is probably due to massive synaptic loss during this period. Dendritic "pruning" and synapse elimination are believed to lead to a more efficient set of connections. [See note 1] Neuron survival and the efficiency of synapses might contribute to the neuroplastic changes that take place in the human central nervous system during childhood, adolescence, and early adulthood.[7, See note 2]

It is suggested that the normal developmental process of dendritic and synaptic pruning might be abnormally accelerated or derailed in schizophrenia.[See note 3] Statistically significant reductions or increases in measured gray or white matter structures are commonly found in children with developmental disorders, although scientists are unsure of the relevance of this finding.[See note 4]

Normal neural pathways may get disrupted, and genetic variations may add and interact to produce the disruption. (Genetic influences are complex and multigenetic in nature, and it is generally accepted that the effects of variations in any one single gene are not likely to be highly influential.) For example, neural development and connectivity in childhood Attention Deficit Hyperactive Disorder (ADHD) is thought to be genetic, although this is still under investigation. Some of these genes may not be broadly involved in the neuro-developmental process; instead, they may interact with specific neural pathways involved in symptom presentation and functional deficits.[8] The abnormal functioning of cortical circuitry in schizophrenia becomes manifest during adolescence when there is an increased demand for proper functioning of the prefrontal cortex.[See note 5]

Structural changes in the brain may play a role in early onset of a disorder.[See note 6] Anterior insular cortex (AIC) degradation may be an area of interest in developmental disorders. The anterior insula is involved in modulating reactivity to salient internal and external stimuli. This attentional executive function is impaired in young psychiatric patients with a broad variety of disorders.[9]

Comparison with Tourette syndrome

Tourette syndrome offers some interesting comparisons. Tourette is considered a genetic developmental disorder with an early onset. Tic behaviors can come on suddenly and there are a number of co-morbid conditions such as OCD.[See note 7] One key hypothesis about Tourette onset is that there are functional abnormalities that develop in the anterior insular cortex (AIC)-anterior cingulate cortex (ACC) system. Production of a sense of inner tension and premonitory urge occurs in the AIC, and the generation of abnormal movements and/or vocalizations occurs in the ACC.

A PET study of tics in Tourette disorder found that activity in both AIC and ACC was significantly correlated with tic occurrence, although many other areas were similarly correlated making specific interpretations difficult. A structural MRI study of brain morphology in familial cases of Tourette disorder reported reduced cortical thickness of the frontal motor, cingulate, and insular cortices, with the degree of cortical thinning correlated with tic severity. There may be delayed or abnormal maturation of areas involved in self-regulation.[10]

# CHAPTER 11
## Emotions Overview

*Anger ... increases tendencies to overlook mitigating details before attributing blame, to perceive ambiguous behavior as hostile, to discount the role of uncontrollable factors in attributing causality, and to punish others for their mistakes.*[1]

"Sound-Rage" is all about emotions, their impact on daily living, and their long term effect on the self in relation to other people. It fuels rapid short-term anger and fury, and sets the stage for developing life-long feelings of powerlessness, vulnerability, and the need for an expanded personal space. There is emotive disgust accompanying thoughts about the source of the trigger. Anxiety arises in the process of trying to scout, avoid, and escape. There is general upset: sufferers worry about "being crazy" and are fretful that their lives are neither normal nor happy.

Emotions have evolutionary value; they can serve to protect us and shield us from harm. It has been theorized that emotional feelings constitute the primary motivation component of mental operations such as decision-making and overt behavior. Rooted in evolution and biology, a basic emotion like anger helps to motivate rapid and often automatic actions "that are critical for adaptive responses to immediate challenges to survival or well being."[2]

Daily unavoidable exposure to common ambient sounds/visuals over which the sufferer has little control results in an ongoing barrage of physical, psychological, and emotional discomfort. The physical discomfort is twofold: 1) there is the impact from the release of hormones and other rapid physiological changes that occur from the autonomic flight response and 2) there is the impact from lingering stress after the trigger-induced response has abated. Psychological discomfort is significant, long-term, and arises as a consequence of long-standing, recurring associations with feeling powerless and vulnerable. Negative thoughts and feelings create barriers to intimacy and trust, disrupting closeness in relationships both personal and professional. Emotions seem to have a life of their own, yet they are intrinsically tied to a person's physical and psychological states. The emotional discomfort of anger and disgust can be mild to severe and extreme, depending on the circumstances surrounding the trigger event.

Emotional processing involves a cascade of physiological and psychological reactions that range from highly automatic and basic to relatively well elaborated and complex. Emotions are altered and enhanced by cognitive appraisals—the thoughts, values, judgments, and beliefs that surround events. There is no way to stop dogs from barking, neighbors blasting the bass of their stereos, or officemates typing on their keyboards. The inability to stop visual, auditory, or olfactory triggers can lead to a tailspin of attempting to gain control and subsequent feelings of powerlessness. Sufferers often report that powerless feelings make them cry long after the trigger is gone. It is well known that crying "is often a manifestation of the struggle to cope."[3]

A sufferer may wear earplugs, headphones, blast white noise, and avoid many places and social interactions in an overt attempt to gain control over the environment, and in a subtle attempt to minimize the inevitable emotional damage. Creating barriers to trigger stimuli is a coping mechanism between the external world and the hard-wiring of the brain in the internal world.

Paradoxically, circumventing exposure to a trigger restricts the sufferer's freedom of movement. When movies, restaurants, exercise classes, seminars, and a host of other quality of life offerings become off limit, there are fewer and fewer opportunities for growth and positive experience. The person ceases to thrive. In attempts to gain control, the ultimate outcome is an increased feeling of powerlessness.

The emotions that arise from a trigger are fast, furious, all consuming, and powerful. Yet anger does not lead to abused dogs or broken computer key boards or smashed stereos. Instead, people flee. What can cause such fury without a fight?

A fundamental premise of this primer is that anger without overt aggression arises as a function of affective pain. It is theorized that the triggers cause affective, non-sensational pain, and it is pain that makes the brain recognize and assess triggers as dangerous and threatening. A discussion of pain, its impact on anger, its relationship with empathy, and its role in the crafting of effective therapies can be found in Chapter 12.

The theory of pain leads to an interesting question: If the trigger creates affective pain and hence suffering, why is there no fear of the source of the trigger? For example, if your brother's constant throat clearing is unbearable, why aren't you afraid of your brother? If his throat clearing is causing suffering and pain and your anger is directed at your brother, why aren't you physically and overtly acting out aggressively?

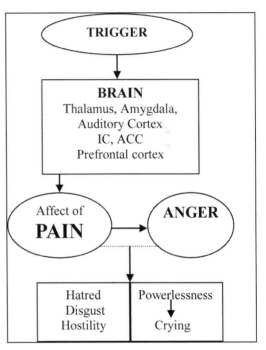

*The answer might be that the circuits that stimulate fear and aggression are not stimulated by "Sound-Rage," whereas the circuits that produce anger are stimulated.*[See note 1]

It could also be argued that the conscious brain has separated, at some level, the source of the trigger (and subsequent pain) and the trigger (pain). The trigger causes the pain; the brother is just the messenger. Physically harming and acting out verbally against the source of the trigger does not alter or mitigate the pain that the trigger causes.

The following chapters further explore anger and disgust and the role of hypervigilance in protecting against danger. The interplay between emotion and cognitive processes contributes to the expansion of triggers and this is presented in Chapter 16.

# CHAPTER 12
## "Sound-Rage" and Pain

*A meta-analysis shows that anger provocation elicits strong changes in systolic and diastolic blood pressure, heart rate, number of skin conductance responses, and muscle activity. The pattern resembles the combined action of adrenaline and noradrenaline. These coordinated changes have a functional value for the pursuit and finally the attainment of the goal of anger: to motivate individuals to avoid pain.[1]*

*The affective-motivational aspects of pain originate in the periphery and suffering is not merely a matter for the neocortex; it is profoundly more ancient and primitive phylogenetically and is reflected in fibre tracts and neural networks throughout the nervous system.[2]*

*The definition provided by the International Association for the Study of Pain is: An unpleasant sensation and emotional experience which is associated with actual or potential tissue damage or is described in terms of such damage and which is expressed in behavior.[3]*

*It truly is a special kind of pain, and no one understands it unless you've got it![4]*

The "Sound-Rage" disorder is differentiated from recognized, defined disorders by its underlying emotion of anger, and the anger's unique manifestation of flight rather than fight. What is behind the emotional thrust that initiates an immediate physiological flight response? What can create (cause) undue rage and feelings of powerlessness? What vulnerability instigates hypervigilance? Why is exposure therapy, successful in the treatment of anxiety disorders such as phobias, ineffective in the treatment of "Sound-Rage"? Pain is the answer to these questions.

My hypothesis is that the trigger stimuli are interpreted and assessed as pain signals. These are affective pain signals; the brain is not responding to bodily sensation. After all, there is no somatovisceral or internal/skeletal harm. External stimuli that comprise the auditory, visual, and olfactory triggers are totally innocuous with regards to tissue damage.

The theory of affective, non-sensation pain is supported by another theory, one that suggests the possibility of a pain network that operates in the total absence of noxious stimulation. This network, comprising emotional and cognitive inputs from higher neural centers, can expand, amplify, and even create pain symptoms. *A mental, rather than physical, experience of pain can originate exclusively within a subject's brain rather than being necessarily dependent on the pathology of peripheral tissue.*[5] This is difficult for many to imagine, but bear in mind its opposite: phantom sensory pain. Phantom pain is actual sensation, most often burning, crushing, or stabbing, in a body part that does not exist. If sensory pain can exist when there is no physical body, then affective pain can exist when there is no bodily harm.

What is pain?
Although it is very difficult to describe in specific, we all certainly know it when we feel it. It's what makes us dread a visit to the dentist or a walk on a slippery path. It has been described as an ache, misery, anguish, discomfort, unbearableness, distress, hurt, or irritation. The scientific literature describes the affective component of pain as "suffering." In effect, suffering is ache, misery, anguish, unbearableness, distress, hurt, irritation and discomfort, all rolled into one.

The physical sensation of pain is the phenomenon and it can be pinpointed. A person can identify the location within or on the body where something hurts. Conceptually, it is very hard to separate the physical sensation of pain from the extreme unpleasantness of pain. This is especially difficult to grasp in "Sound-Rage," where there is no obvious internal or external physical damage. On the face of it, the theory that something hurts when there is no sensation seems illogical and even impossible.

It is actually easier to separate sensation from affect when thinking about pleasure. Picture yourself in a beautiful environment on a gentle, clear day. Your face is warmed by the sun as it tilts upwards to a cloudless, blue sky. The air, fresh and crisp and pollen-free, fills your lungs. Birds are singing in the distance, melodically filling the space with music. These are all sensations of pleasure from the external environment on your physical self. Your body feels a warm temperature, your lungs are filled and stretched, and your muscles are relaxed and pliable and able to move freely. The affect of pleasure is how you feel: comfortable, stable, balanced.

*Scenario 1: Upon hearing or seeing a trigger, signals are sent to the regions of the brain where it interprets the stimuli as pain—not the actual sensation, but rather, its extreme unpleasantness. The emotional response to pain is anger/rage. The physical reaction to a painful altercation or situation is to flee: it is an instinctual reaction to get away from the source of pain. This is a very simplified model of brain-to-pain flight.*

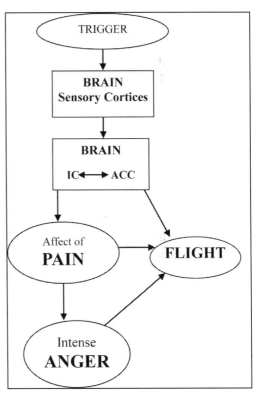

The body has a broad response to pain that includes emotional, neuroendocrine, arousal, autonomic, and somatosensory components.[6] The experience of pain is described along two main axes. The first is the sensory-discriminative dimension that has temporal (time), spatial (space), and intensity properties. The second is the affective-motivational dimension related to the unpleasantness of the stimulus and its behavioral and autonomic arousal reactions.

The affective-motivational component is what is often referred to as "suffering from pain".[7]

Signals originating in peripheral nerves convey nociceptive (pain-neuron) information to the somatosensory cortex and the insula, contributing to sensory aspects such as intensity. The affective dimension of pain relies on neural circuits that are partially anatomically distinct from the sensory dimension system.[8]

The parts of the brain that are activated by the affect of pain are highly interactive and suggestive of a network of interconnected brain regions. These regions are the orbitofrontal cortex (OFC), the anterior cingulate cortex (ACC), anterior insula (IC, insular cortex), amygdala, and periaqueductal gray (PAG).[9] The network facilitates the interaction of flight behaviors, emotional regulation of anger and disgust, and thoughts regarding the circumstances of pain. In other words, the network apprises the "who, what, where, how, and why."

The anterior insular cortex (AIC) and the anterior cingulate cortex (ACC) co-activate when subjects pay attention to subjective experiences of emotion. Positron emission tomography (PET) findings suggest that the AIC is involved in awareness of the unpleasant feeling associated with pain. Signals from cognitive prefrontal areas and emotion-related areas converge in the ACC, which in turn is thought to marshal responses to this unpleasantness. ACC involvement in the pain response is not simply attentional. It is also implicated in the preparation and initiation of autonomic and motor responses to pain—the flight behavior.[10]

Why pain?
Pain serves to warn us of actual or potential tissue damage. It can be pervasive, intrusive, and all-consuming. When a person is in pain, it is the prevalent focus of their immediate consciousness. Think about a time when you have had a terrible headache after a stressful day of work, or a throbbing backache after a day of gardening. As you try to settle into the evening, everything else pales in comparison to the discomfort you are experiencing. It is difficult to think about planning a meal or doing a household chore. The focus is on one's body.

Evolutionarily, pain was often the result of a situation threatening survival, and pairing emotions with pain helped us to create strategies to reduce life-threatening scenarios. If a certain animal is known to bite, it is quite clear that it is best to run away from it. Threatening pain is a stimulus that orients attention to both the source of pain and the potential for escape—what is causing the pain and how to get away from it.[11]

Pain is closely connected to the emotion of anger. Experimental studies using humans as subjects confirm that significant increases in anger (and anger-related thoughts) are triggered by acute physical discomfort; these anger reactions are greater than fearful reactions.[12] The affect of pain (that dog's bite really hurts me) creates a significant interaction between anger (I am enraged at the dog that just bit me) and flight behaviors (I have got to get away from that dog).

Pain explains why exposure therapy doesn't work
The working theory about "Sound-Rage" is that brain's dysfunction arises from a developmental, neurological change that creates a neural environmental in which innocuous auditory, visual, and olfactory stimuli signal danger and pain. This signaling differs from associative learning (or the forming of new neural pathways via plasticity, created from interactive experience). For example, in post traumatic stress disorder (PTSD), a severe traumatic experience sets in motion brain circuitries to cope with danger, with the non-conscious motivation to protect the person from threat. This new circuitry is due to plasticity, the brain's ability to form new neural associations.

In contrast, a developmental disorder like Tourette or "Sound-Rage" has an underlying, developmental dysfunction that did not come about due to an external, traumatic event. Dysfunction may be due to thickening of cortical lining, a reduction of grey matter, changes in chemical neurotransmitters, a breakdown in connections between specific brain regions, among other things. It can be argued that the neural connections in "Sound-Rage" are immutable or "hard-wired," and are exceedingly challenging to modify. This is the reason why a trigger, such as a repetitive lip smacking sound, continues to stimulate the brain's firing of "danger!" and "pain!" year after year, under a wide variety of different circumstances.

The theory that a slow steady exposure to a trigger will shift the neural connections and slowly acclimate the brain to a steady state—an assumption on which extinction therapy is built—does not apply to this disorder. *If the only possible outcome of a hard-wired connection is the signaling of pain, then each exposure will actually reinforce the response rather than diminish it.*

You might ask, "Aren't phobias, like a fear of heights, hard-wired but treated with exposure?" In exposure therapy for certain specific phobias, fear is reduced through repeated exposures to an event that occur without adverse consequences. This learning process is referred to as "extinction," and it is believed that extinction occurs because inhibitory synapses are strengthened.

For example, with acrophobia or fear of heights, extinction is accomplished by exposure through slowly and steadily being situated in progressively higher places. An acrophobic climbs a small hill and looks down. After a certain sense of comfort is met, it is followed by climbing a taller hill. Each time the acrophobic looks down from a new height without adverse consequences, new learning occurs, inhibitory neural pathways are being formed, and fear subsides. This entire process strengthens the inhibition of fear. As fears abate, cognitions (thoughts) about heights also shift.

However, fear arising from exposure to perceived danger, and pain arising from exposure to perceived danger, are very different. Let's take the acrophobia example and tweak it to mimic "Sound-Rage." Suppose that the visual—the sight of looking down—is interpreted by the brain not only as "danger!" but also as "pain!" It is not the actual physical sensation of pain but the extreme unpleasantness or suffering from pain. As you climb that first small hill and look down, there is an immediate reaction. You don't experience the sensation of pain like you would if you put your hand in a fire, but you do experience every other aspect of pain—the body's reaction of extreme discomfort and the need to remove yourself (or your hand) immediately. You might also experience anger. Your brain has recorded this response of discomfort and anger and stored it in memory. As you look down from the next higher hill, your experience of pain is re-lived. Each time you climb higher and look down, the pain occurs. (It wouldn't be surprising if at this point you didn't feel very angry at the exposure therapist!)

Many accounts by sufferers verify that exposure therapy is ineffective and unpleasant. The theory of pain explains why exposure therapy does not work and actually increases upset.

Pain, rage, and feelings of powerlessness
In order to fully appreciate feelings of rage and powerlessness elicited by the syndrome, let's tweak a scenario of a child reacting to a trigger *by adding in the sensation of pain*. The following scenario is from the vantage point of a child who lacks the maturity of certain insights and decision-making that comes with a fully developed pre-frontal cortex.

> *Scenario 2: A young boy eats dinner with his father every night. For the first ten years of the boy's life the boy has never paid attention to his father's eating. One evening he becomes acutely aware of his father's chewing as if hearing it for the first time. The father takes a bite of food -- suddenly the boy feels an explosion in his head. It feels as painful as someone yanking out his front teeth but the searing pain is inside his head, not his mouth. Instinctively, he knows that the sound is causing the pain. Each time his father crunches on a carrot an explosion goes off in his head, creating an intense pain like fire rolled in a tight ball. It is unbearable.*

> *The boy, aware that the pain comes and goes with his father's chewing, screams at him "Stop it. Stop making those sounds."*

*He is beside himself with fury. He has done nothing wrong— he didn't do anything to his father to provoke this attack. It's as if his father doesn't care that his head is about to explode. Within seconds as the chewing continues all he wants to do is get away. The boy is infuriated and enraged. He is in pain and his father keeps eating! It's as if his father is doing this on purpose.*

*As he bolts from the room and out of ear shot the boy notices that the pain is immediately gone. He knows that there is nothing he can do on his own to stop the pain, except to get away from it. He also knows he cannot stop his father from eating.*

*Even though he is in another room now he remains stressed, agitated and furious that his father would cause harm on purpose, especially when there is no way he can protect himself. The boy thinks to himself, "I hate him. I hate him. I hate him."*

In "Sound-Rage," the severe unpleasantness of pain is invasive, particularly since it is outside of the control of the sufferer. Psychologically, it is as if the intrusion by a trigger has crossed a personal boundary. The invasiveness of pain such as in "Sound-Rage" can provoke feelings of powerlessness and lack of control.[13] Neurologically, the contribution of the anterior cingulate cortex (ACC) to the affect of pain (the unpleasantness of pain) seems to be dependent on cognitive factors, such as feeling powerless and vulnerable.[14]

Mimicry, empathy and pain

*Over the years we have tried everything to help him, everyone tells him to ignore it and he can't!! He shows all levels of response to this sound some days he mimics the sound.*[15]

*She also hates when I clear my throat. She will actually clear hers each time I do it!(Basically, she mimics the sound.)*[16]

*I had a compulsion to relieve my irritation by mimicking the sounds he made. Although I was punished harshly for doing this I could not stop myself.*[17]

*I started noticing the symptoms when I was 9 or 10 when I started mimicking my dad sniffing (he has really bad allergies) in a mean way. I guess that was my way of letting my parents know I didn't like the sniffing.*[18]

*mimicking is a way for me to "get back".*[19]

Mimicking behaviour is one of several coping or response schemes evoked by triggers. Mimicry of triggers can begin in either childhood or adulthood, and it appears to serve one of two purposes. Some people report that it is palliative and makes them feel better, while others say they deliberately mimic the source of the trigger as a way of "getting even"; they mimic as an act of defiance or hostility.

Automatic mimicry is defined as unconscious or automatic imitation of facial expressions, gestures, behaviors, speech, and movements. (This is compared to conscious mimicry, where the sufferer is consciously and purposefully making the same sounds as the trigger's source is making.) Vocalizations with accents, rate, and rhythm of speech tend to be automatically mimicked by "interaction partners" or people who closely interact with one another.

Automatic mimicry behaviors are pervasive and systematically related to pro-social attitudes and behavior. It has been argued that mimicry serves as an important communication tool and as an adaptive behavior. It creates a bond or connection between the mimicker and the mimicked. By fostering rapport, it serves to create harmonious relationships.[20]

Social psychology studies have demonstrated that imitation and mimicry are automatic and facilitate empathy.[21] Empathy is sharing and understanding the emotional state of others in relation to oneself.

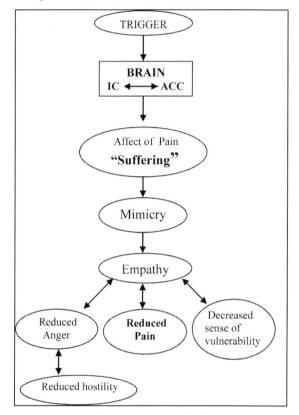

Some components involved in empathy occur without awareness, such as motor mimicry, while others require more complex processing and emotional regulation. Emotional regulation comprises trying to ascertain what another person is feeling, separate from one's own feelings, and requires the cognitive capacity to take the perspective of the other person.

Recent studies on empathy suggest that observation or imagination of another person's state automatically activates a representation of that state in the observer. In repeating triggers (sounds or visuals like finger pointing or leg swinging), a "Sound-Rage" sufferer evaluates—either consciously or non-consciously—the non-hostility of the action.[22]

Empathy makes available to the "Sound-Rage" sufferer a different perspective on the beliefs, motivations, intentions, and emotions of the trigger's source. Through this process, the sufferer gains control over feeling powerless (and perhaps victimized) by assessing that the source of the trigger is not being malicious, hurtful, or invasive. The thought that someone is causing harm and pain intentionally is diminished, reducing the additional stress and threat of the trigger.

Automatic (non-conscious) imitation, empathy, and pain overlap in the neural network including the anterior cingulate cortex (ACC) and the anterior insula cortex (AIC). It is possible that the brain of a "Sound-Rage" sufferer may be automatically mimicking behaviors in a non-conscious attempt to calm or reduce the signaled activation of pain.

In summary, automatic, non-conscious mimicry behavior has its origins in establishing empathy, and empathy centers of the brain overlap with pain centers in the brain. Mimicry may serve to smooth interactions, leading to a reduction in anxiety, anger, and rage. It may be that part of the neurology of empathy is to reduce pain, while the psychological benefit of empathy serves to reduce hostility and anger.

# CHAPTER 13
Anger and Disgust

*It gets so powerful and those emotions build up so hard that I feel my whole body shaking from rage.[1]*

*Anyway, I too fly into blind rages at certain noises. Chewing, smacking, sniffling, cellophane rattling, and keyboards. I don't know when this started, but I'm 24 now and it's gotten worse. It seems like y'all manage to keep it together around strangers, but I can't. I go through the fidget stage, mild irritation stage, then the "lunging" in my chest, before finally destroying something (usually a poor piece of paper that never hurt anyone) or just leaving. It takes a few minutes to calm down after. It's almost worse around my family, because then I either yell or leave, both of which are rude and awful. I feel terrible about it but what can I do? THEY KEEP ON CHEWING. I like to think I'm pretty even keeled except for these few things.[2]*

The emotion of anger/rage is consistently reported as the response to trigger stimuli; fear does not seem to be implicated at all. A valence/intensity model would label both anger and fear similarly as negative and intense, yet people do not confuse the subjective sensations associated with anger and fear.[3] Anger without overt acts of aggression is a lynchpin in understanding this disorder. In understanding how this emotion serves to protect, effective therapies can be crafted.

It is both curious and disappointing that the study of anger unaccompanied by overt acts of aggression is nowhere to be found in the literature on psychiatric disorders. While anger is addressed in Oppositional Defiance Disorder (ODD) and Post Traumatic Stress Disorder (PTSD), there is no formal recognition of dysfunctional anger without aggression in the standard diagnostic scheme of the DSM-IV-TR. (See Chapter 5, What's the Diagnosis.)

## The brain and anger

*An understanding of the brain circuitry underlying anger regulation specifically must necessarily focus on neuroimaging studies that have involved the actual arousal of anger. However, most neuroimaging studies addressing anger-related factors have studied reactions to viewing angry faces or hearing angry speech, methods that do not address anger arousal itself.*[4]

Anger is a challenge to study in the laboratory, due to its very nature of negativity and wide range of intensity, from subtle to extreme. Genuine, real-life affect is especially difficult to simulate under artificial conditions, especially when the prototypical subjects are either "healthy" or a sub-population of college students. Ironically, the anger that is generated by auditory and visual triggers can be easily produced under laboratory conditions by using "Sound-Rage" sufferers as subjects. This could provide fertile grounds for the study of genuine rage.

Basic negative emotions like anger are activated by sub-cortical, sensory-discriminative processes. These processes are thought to arise from the integration of activity in the brain stem, amygdala, insular cortex (IC), anterior cingulated cortex (ACC), and orbito-frontal cortices (OFC).[5] These brain areas also get input from auditory, visual, and olfactory signal assessment and pain signaling centers.

*Anger is part of the human fabric, the emotional component of the fight-or-flight response to threats.*[6]

*If I were to personify anger, I would describe it as a mix between a stalwart castle sentry and an ancient sage. Anger sets your boundaries by walking the perimeter of your soul and keeping an eye on you, the people around you and your environment. If your boundaries are broken anger comes forward to restore your sense of strength and separateness. The questions for anger are: What must be protected and what must be restored?*[7]

Overall, anger as an emotion can be thought of as a response to a threat or the perception of a threat.[8] It is an underlying emotion of the need to flee and escape. Its basic message is one of self-protection. One model of anger posits that all humans have psychological boundaries. When these boundaries are crossed anger is the response to the threat or imperilment of one's place of psychological safety.

Rage arises when the intensity of anger isn't quite enough to deal with the situation, such as when the boundary violations are severe and even life-threatening. "Rage and fury say that enough is more than enough and that all the abuse or boundary violations that went on before end now, in this instant, no questions asked, no excuses accepted."[9] Anger and crossing boundaries play a significant role in "Sound-Rage" by fueling cognitive associations with violation, powerlessness, and invasion of personal space.

Anger as a result of pain: a model

> *Anger stands out as one of the most salient emotional correlates of pain.*[10]

> *Human experimental studies confirm that acute physical discomfort triggers significantly increased anger and anger-related thoughts, even more so than fearful reactions.*[11]

From an evolutionary perspective, an association between emotions and pain might be expected given that pain was often the result of situations threatening the survival of the organism. Along with fear, anger is most likely to be elicited under such threatening circumstances and is an underlying motivator in the flight response. In a rage state, limbic structures, which include amygdala, hippocampal formation, septal area, prefrontal cortex, and anterior cingulate gyrus serve important modulating functions. You've moved from your prefrontal lobe "down to your midbrain, where you can only fight, be in flight or freeze."[12]

My hypothesis is that the reaction of anger is a result of pain, i.e., the triggers are being interpreted as pain signals. (See Chapter 12,

"Sound-Rage" and Pain.) It is not the sensation of pain itself; after all, there is no somatovisceral or internal/skeletal bodily harm. It is the interpretation of all the other attributes of pain rolled into extreme unpleasantness.

The affect of pain, derived from trigger stimuli signaling in the brain, is a neurological dysfunction. It is a result of a developmental change that occurred in the brain. It could be a thickening of a cortical lining, a deterioration of "gray matter" or a breakdown in the connectivity between synapses, neural networks or brain regions (See Chapter 10, A Developmental Disorder), among a host of other possible reasons. There are a number of different models that could account for where in the brain this change occurred (See Chapter 8 on Brain Circuitry). A faulty assessment might have come to the cortex already changed in value due to a malfunctioning early in the auditory cortex, or even earlier in the thalamus or amygdala.

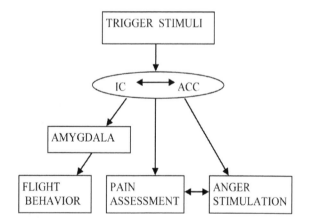

The signal reaches the insular cortex (IC), a center for anger and pain, and rich in connections between the posterior and anterior insular cortex, the auditory cortex, the anterior cingulate cortex (ACC), and the amygdala. (See Chapter 7, The Trigger Brain.) It is the optimal site for integrating all the essential ingredients that comprise a "Sound-Rage" cocktail: auditory inputs, pain assessment, anger stimulation, and all the brain connectivity necessary to initiate motor responses and automatic flight behaviors.

At this point in the processing of the trigger, the brain assesses the signal as "pain!" and as such the trigger is dangerous and a threat to both well-being and survival. As a threat and danger, messages are sent to the amygdala. These messages are, "The sound creates pain. This is dangerous! It's time to get away from the source of pain as quickly as possible!" It is merely a matter of seconds from start to finish, from the time gum chewing is noticed to the time the body's autonomic fleeing response is in full swing.

This disorder presents a double whammy:

1) The pain response, "hard-wired" and highly resistant to change, elicits anger.

2) The automatic response of fleeing is encoded and stored as an implicit memory (sometimes called an emotional memory).

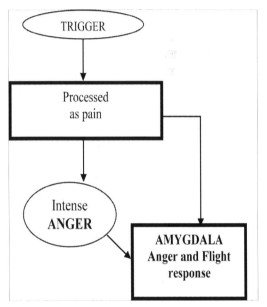

The implicit memory of the physiological flight response is outside of consciousness and controls behavior without explicit awareness of the past learning. It stores all the information it needs about the stimuli and its danger.

It is the brain's implicit memory of an initial trigger that significantly affects the body's autonomic system of flight to the extent that, upon hearing a certain sound, the body knows to flee immediately. None of this is at the cognitive, conscious level.

In implicit memory responses are produced by unconscious processes. The learning that occurs does not depend on conscious awareness, and once the learning has taken place the stimulus does not have to be consciously perceived in order to elicit the conditioned emotional responses.

The sound of a popcorn bag rustling three seats behind you may create a physiological response before you consciously think "Someone behind me is munching on popcorn." It is possible that implicitly processed stimuli activate the amygdala without activating explicit memories or otherwise being represented in consciousness.

How can someone with disorder find any relief? The emotional response which causes distress in daily living is anger. And anger can be mitigated through understanding its response to pain and its relationship to thoughts, values, and beliefs.

Anger without overt acts of aggression

> *I have never physically lashed out, though I have wanted to. Eating and drinking noises drive me up the wall; I have felt pure rage at the sound of someone sucking on a piece of candy, wanted to break the jaw of a gum popper and have come close to throttling moviegoers who don't understand the amount of popcorn they can realistically fit into their mouths. The sound of popcorn squeaking across teeth as someone shoves fistfuls into their face only to chew with their mouth wide open. I have moved seats in theaters. I usually request corner booths in restaurants. Plus, I try to go to noisy eateries to help drown out the sounds.[13]*

> *It's so relieving that other people hate as much as me that they actually get tempted to cry over it like I do. But its not really the chewing sound that annoys me...What really gets at me is for example when someone is eating a piece of hard candy and sucks on it really loudly, constantly smacking their lips in the*

*process. Even covering my ears so I don't hear it isn't enough. It bothers me just to know that they're doing it!!! My dad makes this noise all the time even when he's not eating anything and that drives me up the wall...and I really DO get the urge to smack and yell at people when they do it too! Its almost scary!*[14]

*I literally want to hit someone if they click their gum anywhere near me.*[15]

*On several occasions I have come very close to either punching him square in the face or telling him to chew more quietly but do not. This is mainly because I simply find it excessive/useless to do.*[16]

Anger can be adaptive. As a motivator it physiologically energizes the body to take action against the threat. Yet there remains an incorrect impression that dysfunctional anger always leads to aggression.[17] The reason that anger and aggression are so closely linked is twofold: 1) anger is often difficult to control because of the intense physiological reactions involved in the fight or flight response that it triggers, and 2) anger's expression is often an externalized behavior problem.

Interestingly, in "Sound-Rage" externalized anger manifests as a controlled impulse such as yelling and screaming. Testimonies of controlled anger include clenching ones fist, tearing up paper, or hitting a pillow. Acted out aggression, such as harming others or violently destroying objects, is infrequent. The fantasy or thought of harming others may be prevalent, but is not acted on. In other words, for the vast majority of sufferers, there is anger without overt acts of aggression.

Attentional focus on the source of anger or the person or persons who are creating the trigger might lead to greater self control and a reduced likelihood of open aggression, under some circumstances. Attention to the trigger source appears to be fundamental to the disorder. It is implicated in trigger expansion (see Chapter 16) and therapy (see Chapter 17). "This kind of regulation could happen when people become highly aware of their aroused feelings and think this arousal might influence them to act in socially improper or inappropriate ways."[18]

> *Scenario 1: The boy is sitting in English class and the girl behind him is chewing gum. Every twenty seconds there is a crack sound of the gum popping. He starts counting the gum cracking (one, two, three, four...) and fury builds inside him. He turns around and gives the girl behind him a dirty look. A few minutes later, he turns his head and asks her to please stop chewing so loudly. She agrees yet within one minute she starts chomping her teeth on the gum. He thinks to himself, "I hate her. I want something really bad to happen to her." What he doesn't do is turn around and threaten her.*

> *Scenario 2: A woman hears the clicking of dishes being hand washed in the sink and goes into an immediate rage. She yells and screams, "Stop the noise". She puts her hands over her ears, turns up music so loud as to override and blast out the clicking dish sounds. What she does not do is rush to the kitchen and punch the person washing the dishes. She does not throw the dishes at anyone. There is anger and rage and vengeful thoughts, but no overt aggression. All violence is in her head.*

The fact that there is little if any overt aggression is significant and suggests several things: first, that most people with "Misophonia" or "Sound-Rage" are able to suppress an overt act of aggression or behavioral response of aggression. This ability to focus and suppress aggression speaks to strong regulation and self-control of emotions.

Secondly, there is some mechanism or cognition that allows the sufferer to be aware of the inappropriateness of an aggression response, despite feelings of anger/rage, powerlessness, and disgust, and thoughts such as blame and hatred. On some level, the sufferer is capable of separating the source of the trigger and the trigger itself. This might mean that this type of emotion regulation can be activated automatically, not necessarily as a result of deliberate and conscious functioning.[19] Or, it might signify that anger is purposefully being suppressed, suggesting that neural plasticity is occurring, i.e., inhibitory inputs from the prefrontal cortex getting strengthened, and thus, are inhibiting anger.

Finally, and hypothetically, it is possible that the circuits that stimulate aggression are not stimulated by "Sound-Rage," whereas the circuits that produce anger are stimulated. (See Chapter 11, Emotions Overview.)

On disgust

> *It is as if the entire act of eating has become a vulgar, disgusting act.*[20]

> *GUM, GUM, GUM. I think its disgusting and I don't want to hear people chew it.*[21]

Although not as consistently or frequently reported as anger, a number of sufferers state that they feel disgust—either by the source of the trigger (i.e., "The gum chewer disgusts me") or the behavior of the source (i.e., "The way that person eats is disgusting"). Disgust is considered a response to social violations and in this regard it is more of a cognition or evaluation. [See note 1]

Disgust is thought to serve adaptive functions such as defending against ideological contagions, regulating relationships between social groups, and guarding social order. It is a general rejection system easily extended to a variety of bodily actions and issues motivating avoidance, expulsion, or to otherwise break off contact with the offending entity.[22] We are socialized by our disgust, and in turn, use it to socialize others. By declaring a habit "disgusting," we are attempting to stop people from doing something that is considered socially undesirable.[23]

# CHAPTER 14
## Hypervigilance and Attention to Danger

*It can get to the point where I can tell if someone has food in their mouth even if they're in another room.*[1]

*I will fly into an uncontrollable rage at the constant clacking of a spoon when someone is eating cereal, they can be across the house three rooms away, with walls and doors in between - AND I CAN STILL HEAR EVERYTHING!*[2]

*When I'm at the movies and someone is chewing popcorn anywhere in the movie theater it bothers me so much I can't pay attention to the movie.*[3]

*There is a fellow graduate student in my lab who eats noisily and also breathes very heavily. I make a point not to sit next to him at lab meetings or I can't pay attention to the presenter.*[4]

Sufferers experience two behaviors also found in people who have Post Traumatic Stress Disorder (PTSD) or chronic pain conditions: selective attention and hypervigilance. Both behaviors are very closely related and are often used synonymously. Selective attention is the tendency of the body to orient attention and resources to specific stimuli. Hypervigilance refers to an enhanced state of sensory sensitivity, plus heightened attention to environmental threat detection and avoidance.

In general, all human beings possess selective attention capabilities. Tremendous amounts of stimulation come at us all the time and from all directions. Our brains focus on the objects and people most relevant to our lives or well being at any given time, and work to filter out the rest. This pattern of being attuned to danger is a form of protection from threat or death. An efficient detection of threat is crucial for survival and requires an appropriate allocation of attentional resources toward the location of potential danger.

Selective attention capability is critical: if we are overwhelmed by the traffic lights, honking horns, and throngs of pedestrians on a busy city street, we might miss an oncoming bus heading straight for us. Our human brain is acclimated towards scanning, responding to, and becoming sensitized to signals of danger. We are primed to be on the lookout for danger.[See note 1] This preferential tendency becomes a way of being for people with "Sound-Rage." In an otherwise quiet environment, the sufferer seeks out or scouts for potential triggers.

In psychiatric disorders where the brain senses danger, there is purposeful scanning of the external environment for signs of threat. fMRI data suggest that negative emotional stimuli not only draw attention, but hold that attention more strongly than neutral or positive stimuli.[5] This is hypervigilance, which sensitizes the brain to scan and evaluate stimuli that may endanger well-being. It is intuitively logical that if a particular trigger causes pain, you will work very hard to avoid it. In order to avoid it you must know where it is, and that may require being on constant lookout.

The persistence in looking for a trigger can change your tendency to detect noxious sensations.[6] Even if the trigger is fleeting, you will capture it, focus on it, input its information, and be subjected to subsequent pain. The extent of hypervigilance is exacerbated because most triggers randomly occur throughout the day, in all walks of life.

<u>How hypervigilance harms the sufferer: seek and ye shall find.</u>
Ongoing attention to triggers is most often at the expense of focusing on other higher-cognitive functions. It serves to keep the person feeling safe from threat, but diverts necessary focus on tasks at hand. For example, Raul is about to take a test in school. As the class gets settled in, he looks around the room seeking gum chewers, students with colds, and people who exhibit nervous twitches, such as finger tapping on the desk or kicking the leg of the chair in front of them. Rather than relaxing and preparing for the upcoming exam, he is expending mental energy, alerting arousal systems, and feeding anxiety that a trigger source will be found. It is no wonder that through time, hypervigilance itself creates a host of ancillary social and psychological issues.

The detection of emotionally laden stimuli signalling "danger!" and "pain!" is followed by altered thresholds for the detection of other sources of threat, and enhanced vigilance to such signals. Arousal seeks stimuli and stimuli create arousal in a symbiotic dance that keeps the sufferer on watch at all times. The amygdala, hippocampus, and anterior insula (areas implicated in pain, danger, and the evaluation of valence of auditory, visual, and olfactory sensory information) respond preferentially to signals of danger.[7]

The key problem with selective attention as it relates to "Sound-Rage" is that once stimulated by triggers, the brain becomes sensitized and develops a hyper-aroused state. In a hyper-aroused condition there does not necessarily have to be a real trigger stimulus in order to create a stress reaction. Sensory areas of the cortex can be activated in the absence of an external stimulus, either as a result of attention or by imagining a visual or auditory stimulus.[8]

Arousal can enhance the sensitivity of visual and auditory cortex to stimuli, drawing attention to triggers that normally would be ignored. Extreme anger from pain not only influences how a person might interpret visual stimuli, but might also determine what a person will detect in the first place. It is possible that a "Sound-Rage" sufferer might be more likely to be visually aware of other brief visual events or have an enhanced ability to detect objects that would otherwise blend into their background.

*Hypervigilance creates an arousal state that is primed and ready for a trigger. It seeks a trigger, however visually distant or faint. It aids and abets the expansion of triggers. In seeking to protect itself from danger, the "Sound-Rage" brain inadvertently finds a hostile environment.*

# CHAPTER 15
Cognition: How the Brain Thinks about Triggers

*Sensory information undergoes extensive associative elaboration and attentional modulation as it becomes incorporated into the texture of cognition.*[1]

*If it's an unattended animal I start thinking negative tirades about how inconsiderate the owner is, and the thoughts actually make it much worse.*[2]

Introduction
Triggers elicit an extreme anger response. (This primer suggests that the anger is due to the brain's interpretation of the trigger signals as "pain"). Thoughts, beliefs, values, judgments, and decisions are created through time as a result of the relationship between a trigger and the brain's response. The source of the trigger, the situation or interaction, and the external physical environment, or the who-what-and-where, all have relevance in how we think about triggers.

Although a trigger has an immediate effect on the sufferer, it is the cognitions, the potpourri of thought, that have an even greater, longer lasting impact. Our beliefs are what we live by. If we feel powerless, we extend that belief to how we operate in the world both personally and professionally. If we feel vulnerable, we restrict our intimacy with other people. If we feel violated, we lose our trust. If we judge others as "disgusting" and "rude," we remove otherwise well-intended people from our lives. And if we feel bombarded by threat, we expand our need for personal space.

Emotions such as anger, and cognition comprising thoughts, values, opinions, and impressions, have separate features and functions, but their influences are interactive and highly integrated in the brain. Our full understanding of the subtleties and complexity of emotion-cognition interactions is limited, despite theories in psychology that support the interactive dynamic. Affective states arising from visceral, internal bodily reactions called "bottom-up processes" may be primed by cognitive appraisals or "top-down processes" and these mechanisms mutually reinforce one another.[3]

In the laboratory, cognitive events such as thoughts, memories, and beliefs might be studied separately from emotional events. Yet in the real world of how the brain functions, the distinction between how you feel about a situation and what you think about a situation is hazy. Brain structures that regulate and modulate emotions, such as the amygdala, the insular cortex, the anterior cingulate cortex, and other connected brain regions have an impact on cognitive processing from early attention allocation through perceptual processing to memory. It is exceedingly difficult to fully separate feeling and thinking.[4]

Many theorists suggest that the distinction between cognitive activity and emotional experience is probably better conceptualized as a gradient, rather than two independent, interacting systems. If anger is immediate and automatic, how does that contribute to the thoughts we have about the triggers and the people who create the triggers? In turn, how do those thoughts shape our reactions, not only to the triggers themselves, but to the people and environment that surround us?

Emotion has substantial and measurable effects on cognition and action when the stimulus has personal significance, like the sound of constant sniffing or throat clearing. This suggests that the emotions of anger and rage, in the face of a perceived threat that is immediate, dangerous, and painful, will alter or shape the cognitions or thoughts that accompany the discomfort.[5]

> *Scenario 1: You are sitting in your kitchen when you mother starts eating a salad. You immediately feel rage. In anger, you think, "I hate her for eating like a pig!" You then begin to feel as if your mother is making noise on purpose. You begin to believe that the noise bothers you because of your mother. This fuels your anger even more.*

## Thoughts and triggers

Even in early youth, a time when a person lacks a mature prefrontal cortex necessary for executive functioning and control, the conscious thinking brain is a problem solver. When a sufferer of any age is confronted by a fundamental dilemma, such as determining the connection between an immediate fleeing response and the external world, the cognitive self seeks to reconcile the relationship between feeling danger and knowing that there is no real danger. [See note 1] The formulation of opinions and assessments about the triggers, decisions regarding how to avoid them, judgments about the sources of the triggers (the people who create them), and thoughts regarding blame and recriminations, are all attempts to make sense of and cohabitate with the disorder in daily living.

> *Scenario 2: The young boy is in class and the girl behind him is chewing gum. He is getting agitated and disturbed. He thinks to himself, "I wish she would just shut up. She is a trouble-maker." The young boy cannot focus on the teacher and is getting visibly upset. He wants to leave the room, but cannot explain to the teacher why, because he knows the teacher will not understand how the girl is bothering him. She won't believe him that the little girl is chewing on purpose and that the sound makes him really angry.*

Cognitions shape how we perceive the world and our place in it, and have as much an impact on our overall quality of life as does the intensity of "Sound-Rage." Unfortunately, many of the underlying cognitions we have about ourselves and the people around us are skewed by looking through the tinted lens of extreme discomfort.

## Examples of cognitive assessments

> *Scenario 3: I'm going to try and be rational. The problem is the noise makers' sense of entitlement and their obvious disrespect for public places. People can control the noises they make. Popping gum, smacking their lips, and breathing in and out so everyone else can hear them. They can control those noises! And when they make those noises in places where we are*

> *all stuck together it is basically saying "I am more important than you. My pleasure, my comfort, I don't care about you. It's all about me." It's an entitlement thing. How can we live if there are no rules in society? This is all rudeness and it insults me and fills me with absolute rage. Maybe I have a heightened sense of what is civil and proper and respect for other people. I like animals and their noises only infuriate me when the owners show absolute disrespect by allowing their animals to bark all night.*

Here the sufferer believes that his/her rage reaction to triggers, such as popping gum and heavy breathing, is in response to inappropriate societal behaviors of other people. In keeping with that belief, they justify their reaction to animal-created triggers by associating the animal sounds with human behaviors. The sufferer's assessments seek to explain, justify, or make sense of an otherwise non-conscious autonomic reaction to innocuous stimuli through a series of judgments about other people's motivations. This person has concluded that selfishness, entitlement, and disrespect are the necessary ingredients to make an innocuous sound become a trigger. The sufferer has created a story about what a social norm should be, and makes assumptions about the thoughts, feelings, and motivations of other people.

> *Scenario 4: There are many things I can't stand but I really hate doors slamming and the sounds on a computer. These noises are illegal, I mean, they shouldn't happen in the library. It makes it impossible for me to study there. When I am in the supermarket there is a ton of noise, but it doesn't bother me because the supermarket is supposed to be noisy. If I'm reading in the library and people start working on their laptops I get very angry, it's supposed to be quiet in here. And don't start talking on your whispering on your phone either.*

This sufferer has evaluated and assessed that certain stimuli become triggers because of the environment in which they occur. They have formed the cognition that creating a trigger stimulus in certain environments is a violation ("illegal"). In a quiet environment, auditory or visual triggers feel like a potent violation because they cross a personal space boundary wherein "quiet" is the expectation.

> *Scenario 5: The rudest thing I have ever heard is people chomping away on gum with their mouths open. I think they do it intentionally—I can stare at them or give them dirty looks when they chew and they keep on doing it. Intentional and rude! They have no respect and do not care about anyone but themselves. It's called etiquette, not eating like a cow. The second rudest thing is people making sounds by texting and clicking on their keyboard! I somehow feel that people are making these noises almost on purpose.*

The sufferer assessed that his/her anger is in response to the motivation(s) of the source of the trigger, and formed judgments about the motivations. The evaluation that the source is rude is a common evaluation among sufferers. Again, the brain is trying to resolve the relationship between stimulus (a rude person is being disrespectful or a person is intentionally trying to make a sufferer angry) and response (rage).

> *Scenario 6: My husband is an adult and knows I dislike how he eats. Tonight he is in bed, licking a spoon and eating a huge bowl of ice cream, smacking his lips. I can tolerate our kids eating, they are just learning. But my husband should know better. I have told him to stop eating like a pig and he says he is just trying to enjoy the treat. I do not know how to tolerate people who eat like pigs.*

The sufferer assessed that her anger is in response to the eating behaviors of the source. The behaviors are the way someone makes a particular sound and the situations/environments in which they eat. It is common for many sufferers to assess trigger sources as eating their snacks and meals "like a pig," implying that if the sources ate "properly," it would not bother the sufferer.

### Cognition: when the source matters

> *I drive myself crazy with this, it's so frustrating. I heard an annoying wet clicking sound the other day and I thought it was my coworker chewing, and I started to grind my teeth with rage...then I figured out she was punching holes in foam. Suddenly the noise didn't annoy me, which is ridiculous. A noise is a noise is a noise.* [6]

The source of the trigger plays a significant role in the "Sound-Rage" disorder. It can mean the difference between immediate arousal and rage or a quick calming of one's physiological state. Onset of the disorder is in late childhood/early adolescence, and it follows that the first or original trigger source is most likely a parent, sibling, or someone with whom the sufferer has daily contact. Through time, the source of the trigger becomes increasingly relevant with respect to the severity of the response to the stimuli.

One possibility is that associated cognitions about the source of the trigger modify the neural response to the trigger, in circuits that process salience (importance) and valence (level of unpleasantness) of the stimuli. One such associated cognition may be a value.

A value cognition could be as simple as "good" or "bad." We routinely apply values about the behaviors of those who are closest to us. With regards to "Sound-Rage," a value might 1) the source has the potential to harm me, 2) the source is a pain-causing object or, 3) the source purposely invades/violates my personal space.

When these values are assigned to the source of the trigger, they become a powerful modulator in the firing of signals in the insular cortex-anterior cingulate cortex region of the brain. Simultaneously, the non-conscious brain assesses the trigger signal, the source, and the source's value, and arrives at: this person is causing pain.

At some point after repeated experiences, the brain associates values—not necessarily the source itself—with the trigger stimuli. Thus, if a particular person is making a clicking sound, it represents "danger!" and the brain is aroused. If it's the wind making the clicking sound, the brain remains calm.

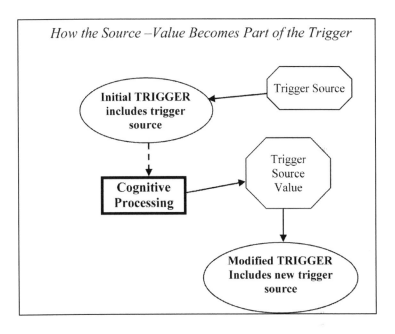

What seems to have transpired is that the person with "Sound-Rage" has associated values with the source rather than with just the actual trigger, so that the source itself has become an integral component of the trigger's signal. This may explain, in part, why a sufferer starts a rage response when they think the sound is popping gum (i.e., the source is the person sitting next to you), but immediately calms when it is discovered that the sound is coming from something altogether different, such as a balloon popping.

It is being postulated that cognitions (i.e., beliefs, assessments, values, and judgments) can create associations between an original trigger and external phenomenon (i.e., who created the trigger, what was the situation, and what was the environment). This can result in the expansion of triggers; it can also result in a reduced response to a trigger.

A trigger is thought to be hard-wired; signals of danger and pain will occur non-consciously and automatically. The relationship between the trigger and its assessment will be resistant to change. Nevertheless, conscious thought can modify many neural pathways and strengthen inhibitory circuits, thus reducing both the intensity and impact of triggers. This is addressed further in Chapter 17 on therapies.

Cognition and the expansion of triggers
As a child matures into adolescence, there is a shift in how the brain processes emotional events. The frontal lobe region responsible for thoughts, beliefs, values, and conceptualizations becomes increasingly engaged in emotional control. What does this mean for "Sound-Rage"?

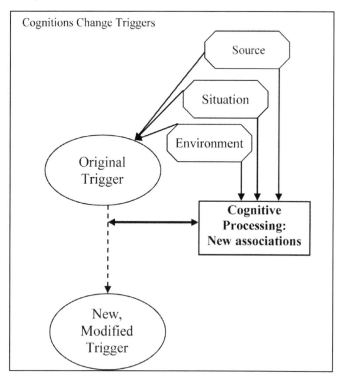

We know that cognition adds input to the non-conscious, neurobiological processing of auditory, visual, and olfactory stimuli. Associations, thoughts, and other related evaluations develop as the person gets older.[7] This forebodes that as a sufferer ages, the triggers will continue to get shaped and modified, further expanding the repertoire of stimuli that create a "danger" and "pain" threat.

In other words, through time, the types and number of triggers are apt to increase. (A more comprehensive discussion is made in Chapter 16 on trigger expansion.) This has two implications: 1) Early intervention might prevent/preclude the expansion of triggers and 2) As a person matures, therapeutic techniques involving emotion regulation through cognition can be effective in reducing trigger expansion or trigger severity.

The cognition of hatred

*If we have suffered or expect to suffer some wilful injury from a man, or if he is in any way offensive to us, we dislike him; and dislike easily rises into hatred. Such feelings, if experienced in a moderate degree, are not clearly expressed by any movement of the body or features, excepting perhaps by a certain gravity of behaviour, or by some ill temper. Few individuals, however, can long reflect about a hated person, without feeling and exhibiting signs of indignation or rage. A man, for instance, may know that his life is in the extremest peril, and may strongly desire to save if; yet, as Louis XVI. said, when surrounded by a fierce mob, "Am I afraid? feel my pulse." So a man may intensely hate another, but until his bodily frame is affected, he cannot be said to be enraged. Charles Darwin.[8]*

*Hatred is an intense flare of rage from boundary devastation and the near complete loss of equilibrium. It is not dislike or fear.[9]*

*I will literally sit there with my fingers in my ears. I hide my parents gum because they chew it so damn loudly and I get really really annoyed at them! I hate it when someones cutlery hits their teeth, I hate when people are eating apples beside me and when people make these sounds I automatically hate them. They think I'm the one being rude when it's them (I swear deliberatley) making the sounds.*[10]

Many sufferers talk about hate; they hate the sound of chewing, but also equate hatred with their feeling toward the source of the trigger. Is hatred a thought-derived affect that arises from anger? It motivates avoidance of specific targets, and in this regard it may serve as a form of protection. It has been proposed that hatred originates from disgust, results from anger and fear, and devalues others based on contempt.[11] Hatred is a perceptual framework focused on the sources of triggers, and is one of the more unfortunate consequences of the disorder.

# CHAPTER 16
Trigger Expansion

If "Sound-Rage" were a reaction to just one particular sound made by one particular person, it would be manageable. Unfortunately, trigger expansion is a key component of this disorder. It expands in sensory modality, from sound to sight to smell, creating a multitude of daily onslaughts that are virtually impossible to avoid. These expanded triggers are immediate sharp spikes of "danger!" and "pain!"

Cross-modality from auditory to visual, and from a stationary visual to a motion visual, occurs without conscious thought. From the initial onset of one or two mainly auditory triggers to a lifetime of avoiding snifflers, schlurpers, finger pointers, and leg shakers, the insidiousness of the syndrome comes from the steady building of sounds, visuals, and smells to avoid.

Sufferers across the board engage in hypervigilant attention to sources, situations and environments where triggers might occur. (See Chapter 14 on hypervigilance.) Hypervigilance can begin as a cognitive process in which an individual concerned about particular threats closely monitors environmental conditions. This acute attention can alter the sensitivity of the brain to trigger stimuli. And through these changes in sensitivity, the brain is primed to take in, modify, and expand triggers.

Hypervigilance feeds the pathology of the brain. This was aptly demonstrated in an interesting experiment in which monkeys heard sounds while concomitantly tapping their fingers. Some monkeys received juice when responding to a sound, while the others were taught to pay attention to what they feel on their fingers. The brains of the two groups of monkeys were compared after six weeks. The researchers found brain changes based on what the monkeys paid attention to, despite being subjected to both sound and finger stimulation. Monkeys who paid attention to their fingers had an expansion in the somatosensory cortex, but no changes elsewhere. Monkeys who paid attention to sound had increased their auditory cortex region, but had no changes elsewhere.[1]

Sustained, emotionally charged attention to particular trigger sources and events increases the amplification of the response to the triggers over time.[2] Paying attention to a particular target ramps up the activity of the neurons that process and register the target, while quelling the activity of other neurons. Although the information that is reaching the brain has not changed—the motion of the leg shaking is the same, the sound of a gum popping has not intensified—the neurological activity associated with processing that information is heightened.

The neurological expansion of triggers, discussed here and in Chapter 9 on multi-sensory processing, can be thought of as a non-conscious process built into the physiology of the brain. Numerous subcortical structures are involved in multisensory processing, including the thalamus and the amygdala. Cortical operations such as those carried out by primary sensory regions, such as the auditory cortex and visual cortex, are also shaped by inputs from more than one sensory modality.

As we learn more about how signals fire in the brain, we uncover increasing evidence that neurons in areas formerly considered unisensory, like the auditory cortex, actually exhibit multisensory characteristics.[3]

Sight, sound, smell, touch, and taste converge early in the processing scheme. It is becoming more and more apparent that the brain does not process any one external stimulus in isolation.

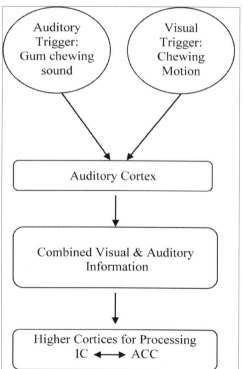

With the integration of different sensory modalities, it is not surprising that a sound trigger can rapidly become a visual trigger that elicits a signal of danger. In fact "prominent non-auditory stimuli are generated before auditory stimulus onset because some visible or palpable action is required to produce a sound."[4]

Visual information can make the auditory information stand out by sensitizing the brain to the auditory stimuli and putting both visual and auditory information together into storage as a memory. For example, opening a gum wrapper occurs before chewing begins, and for most vocalizations like chewing sounds, lip and/or facial movements precede sounds. It is acknowledged by most sufferers that their systems become aroused when seeing someone pull out a stick of gum or hearing a gum wrapper being crinkled. Just the sight of someone chewing without any accompanying sound can instigate an arousal state.

An auditory phenomenon, such as the clicking of a pen, is accompanied by the visual stimuli. The person holding the pen, moving their fingers on the pen, clicking down on the top of the pen, are common visuals. When the visual information comes into the brain, those pieces of data are connected in a brain region where neural activity of two or more senses are integrated. The person holding the pen provides a piece of information that is connected to the 'click-click-click' sound of the pen top being pressed down. The motion of the finger holding the pen and pressing down on the pen top is part of the sensory information. All of these pieces of data connect and contribute to the salience of the sound, i.e., how much that particular sound stands out from all the other pieces of stimuli bombarding the body.

It is generally acknowledged that viewing the event that generates the auditory stimulus increases the subjective intensity of auditory sensation. For example, sitting in a meeting and watching someone "fidget" with a pen increases the arousal that accompanies the sound that the pen makes when it is clicked on and off, even though the visual of a person holding the pen has no immediate behavioral relevance.[5] Watching a person eat actually makes the auditory experience more pervasive and intense. A typical sufferer-experience would be, "I can't even stand to look at people chewing on television. Even if I turn the volume down, I can't watch because I can imagine what it sounds like."

New auditory–visual perceptual associations can be acquired based on brief exposure to correlated auditory and visual coincidences, even in adult sensory systems.[6] If a visual is associated with a trigger sound, the brain will process this information together into a single, relevant view of the value of the auditory or visual information, even if the visual does not contribute to the salience of the sound.

The sound-visual associations that occur neurologically in the brain can be made at any age, allowing for the expansion of triggers to expand the repertoire of danger! pain! signals throughout one's life. For some people it may be a matter of years before new triggers occur; for others, it may be a much briefer period of time. Early intervention is critical in keeping trigger expansion at bay. This is of critical importance to modifying associations and reducing their impact, which is discussed in the next chapter on therapy.

Multi-modal processing of a trigger sound occurs in the first ports-of-call in the brain, such as the thalamus, and in the low sensory cortical regions, such as the auditory cortex. As you recall from earlier chapters, the memories formed here are non-conscious and inaccessible. It is readily understandable how the sound of clanking dishes and the visual of silverware scraping against teeth are integrated. They are both part of the environmental picture when a chewing sound was first processed as "danger!" and "pain!"

The sharp clicking sound of a nail clipper merges with the basic visual information, such as the person's hand and fingers on the nail clipper, in the auditory cortex. Maybe this is the tipping point, beyond which the trigger information is merged and morphed into new triggers. Even the motion of the fingers may be a part of the multi-modal processing.

Studies have found that when people listen to recognizable sounds, regions of the cortex implicated in high-level visual processing of complex biological motion are activated. Stimulated signals may represent 'action' knowledge relating to how the sounds are produced, and the brain may use these signals to recognize familiar environmental sound-sources.[7]

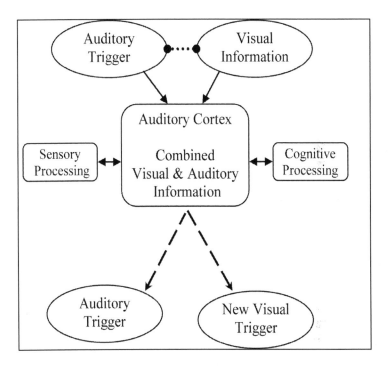

*Initially the auditory and visual stimuli are not associated with each other in the brain, and therefore the association needs to be established by repeated exposure to coupled stimuli. The establishment of the association enables the auditory stimulus to enhance the processing of the visual stimulus (and vice versa.) This improves performance in detection/ discrimination in the presence of the coupled stimuli. Once this multisensory association is established, the pairing of the auditory–visual stimuli will not only*

*improve processing at the time of stimulation, but will also lead to plasticity within and between the sensory representations of these associated features. This will produce the facilitation and enhancement that occurs in the absence of multisensory stimulation.*

*This could be the result of visual and multisensory representations eventually becoming equivalent, where exposure to a unisensory stimulus could invoke the multisensory representation, without the need for multisensory stimulation. It is possible that this multisensory facilitation of unisensory learning is only possible for auditory and visual features that are ecologically associated, such as auditory and visual motion, or lip movements and voice, etc. These ecologically valid associations may be distinct due to hardwired connectivity in the brain.* [8]

The brain takes in information from different parts of the environment. Some stimuli get processed as a warning of threat and are routed through neural pathways to different brain regions. Through time, the brain uses higher reasoning centers to make associations, connecting ambiance (aspects of the external environment), feelings (hatred, powerlessness), and emotions (disgust) with danger and pain. In "Sound-Rage," harmless stimuli get misidentified as threats, stimulating feelings and responses in an inappropriate manner.

<u>New triggers, new associations, new issues</u>
Whether triggers expand through neurological mechanisms of multisensory processing, or are learned through association between stimuli and response, the outcome is the same: an expanded repertoire of external phenomena creates an anger experience.

It is hypothesized that the anger response is generated from the brain interpreting the signals as the valenced unpleasantness of pain. Through time, repeated exposure to pain and anger creates another fundamental shift that has an impact on one's psychological health. The emotional feelings that arise from the trigger-to-pain paradigm, such as anxiousness, tension, and the need for an expanded personal space, take on a life of their own. New triggers that arise through time become associated with how they make a sufferer feel.

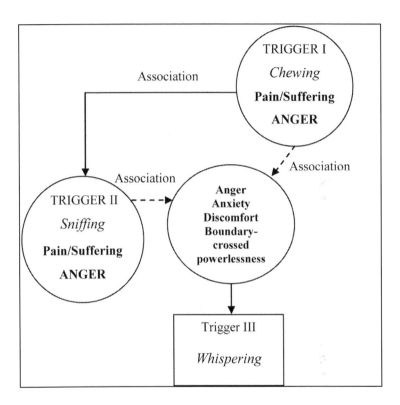

This may be different from the association of "danger!" and "pain!" and the need to flee that are typical of the first, original auditory triggers. New triggers, such as the visible shaking leg motion of a person sitting next to a sufferer, may cause discomfort, despair, and a host of other feelings and cognitions.

There may not be the same level of intensity of anger; anger arises, but it may or may not be from the "pain!" interpretation of the stimuli signals. It may be that the pain assessments of new triggers are not as intense or unpleasant as the assessment of an original trigger.

"Sound-Rage" has an overwhelming impact on the quality of life. Psychiatric behavioral reactions of intense rage without aggression make way for a host of psychological reactions that terminate conversation, compassion, intimacy, and relationships. The psychological aspects of trigger expansion exacerbate the discomfort of the symptoms and lead to unhealthy, self-defeating behaviors.

Therapy can help ameliorate the impact of expanded triggers and is discussed in the next chapter.

# CHAPTER 17
## Therapies

*I have had my problem since I can remember (small child). It started mostly with eating noises (smacking lips mostly). As I got older, it got worse. It has controlled my life. I can't go to the movies unless I get there early to get a seat in the back on the end. I have to get up and move in church when someone is chewing gum or an older person is making involuntary mouth noises over and over. I can't ride in a car unless I feel safe that no one will be eating ... I have tried to get help for this since I started therapy in 1987 I have tried to get rid of my fear for 20 years. I have done every kind of counseling and therapy (from group to individual, meditation, etc.). The psychiatrists and therapists that I have encountered over all these years have never been able to help me with this and haven't heard of anything as extreme as my problem is. I'm wondering if anyone else feels like I do and if anyone has ever gotten any relief. Most of the therapists have said that it could and probably should be related to some type of childhood sexual abuse. I have had a diagnosis of depression since 1989 and extreme anxiety lately.[1]*

*I have been on so many different types of antidepressants in all these years that I can't even remember all of them.[2]*

*I'm on various medications, and always carry earplugs with me. What is the most effective solution for this type of Sound Sensitivity? Is surgery an option? Help.[3]*

*I take anti-anxiety medication but all that really helps me with is controlling my rage.[4]*

*I have seen several family doctors, psychiatrists and psychologists, with no help. I have taken several different anti-depression medications and anti-anxiety medications.*[5]

*My therapist thought the anger I developed in response to chewing sounds was related to unsolved anger towards my step-father (the abuser). That sounded like a logical cause for me. Still, many years later I've successfully dealt with issues related to sexual abuse but continue to face feelings of rage associated with sounds.*[6]

*I can't go a day without earplugs.*[7]

Introduction

After the neurobiology of the disorder has been tentatively identified and the processes for trigger expansion have been described, the next and foremost question is "Is there a cure?" Sadly, the answer is no. At this time, there are no medical therapies, procedures, or protocols for the disorder.

Likewise, there are no pharmacological solutions. Medications have little practical application in lessening the impact of triggers on anger and pain. There are no prescription drugs that stop the neurological responses to trigger stimuli. Anti-depressants such as serotonin reuptake inhibitors will help to mitigate the severity of depression and anxiety. They may offer the sufferer a calmer, less aroused system, and this may play a role in managing and coping with "Sound-Rage," but will not cure it.

The fact that there is no cure comes as a great disappointment, and adds fuel to hopelessness for many people who have lived with this disorder for years and have attempted many different forms of therapy. Throughout their lives, adult sufferers have been acutely stigmatized by having a disorder that is neither identified nor recognized by the medical and psychiatric communities and the general public. Under a veil of anger, outburst, and flight, many have spent years attempting to negotiate intimate relationships with family and friends without the benefit of the understanding, compassion, and support that typically are given to people who have a known neurological or psychiatric disorder.

The fact that there is no cure presents an overwhelming sense of uncertainly about the future for the people who have children or loved ones with this disorder, and who have been witness to the intense anguish that it creates. Children are confused and frightened by their symptoms and associated feelings. When aroused, they are in a highly agitated state of anger; after arousal, they may feel sadness, shame, and remorse. It is heart-wrenching for parents to watch their children undergo these transformations and equally heart-breaking to know that they cannot make the problem go away.

The desire for a cure is exacerbated by the reality that daily living is under constant disruption. Stress and conflict in trying to normalize a difficult home environment diminishes everyone's emotional resources. As sufferers, the disorder limits our possibilities for anger-free experiences and puts us in adversarial roles with the people closest to us. As caregivers, we may lack the knowledge, skills, and consistent calm necessary to help sufferers adjust to their physiological states of arousal, to find a place of comfort, and to de-activate from rage. Even in well-intended families, many households subsist on hostility born of daily anger. Even well-intended caregivers may remain incredulous that a person can feel such anger at something as harmless as a sniff.

Managing the disorder
The following suggestions for managing "Sound-Rage" focus specifically on reducing the severity of the symptoms of the disorder. These practices home in on the trigger-response relationship and the emotional and physical responses that come from the brain's interpretation of trigger signals as danger and pain. The suggestions do not reflect or address the myriad ancillary issues that sufferers may be facing. They do not address unresolved familial issues— either connected to or separate from "Sound-Rage." And they do not address the feelings of guilt, shame, confusion, vulnerability, and powerlessness that skew social interactions and create barriers to intimacy and trust.

The following suggestions are not meant to help with personal or social relationships, affective disorders such as depression, or other diagnosed conditions such as post traumatic stress disorder. Talk therapy, psychoanalysis, and a host of other therapeutic regimens exist that address these types of issues.

After accepting that there is no cure the next question is, "Can I learn to live with this?" The answer is yes, but there are a number of caveats. One of the key goals of managing the disorder is changing the relationships between the stimuli, the physiological and emotional responses, and the cognitions. This is accomplished by making new associations with the triggers and changing the neural pathways in the brain.

And changing neural pathways in the brain is not an easy task. Synaptic connectivity tends to be very stable in the limbic system, a system that we have seen is highly implicated in the "Sound-Rage" disorder. We know that plasticity in the brain exists and that neural patterns do change, but the limbic system is fairly resistant to change induced by cognitive processes.

Nevertheless, change can be accomplished; synapses in the limbic system can be altered, but it requires a lot of mental effort to induce plasticity. Since the limbic system gets feedback from higher-order cortical areas, strengthening this feedback can help control symptoms. There are at least three things that help the brain to form new pathways: commitment to daily practices for improvement, social support, and optimism. To that end:

1) You must have diligence. The underlying neurological dysfunction that signals the anger response cannot be corrected, but the severity and intensity of its effect can be managed through diligent practice of a number of different activities. The key is persistent attention, on a daily basis, to the therapeutic practices that you choose. Like dealing with diabetes, each and every day requires thoughtful commitment to managing the disorder. There are long term gains and benefits, but it requires a daily regimen.

2) You must accept that it takes a concerted amount of emotional and psychological energy to focus on managing the disorder. For caregivers, it requires a great deal of emotional and psychological energy to offer consistent and unconditional support despite being vulnerable as the object of someone's anger.

For sufferers, it requires discipline and concentration to apply energy resources necessary for changing neural pathways in the brain. Even if you are in an environment that is initiating a trigger-induced arousal, you must remind yourself of your commitment to changing your thoughts about the trigger and its source. This attempt, despite concurrent anger and the need to remove yourself quickly, is actually quite important because it takes repetition and time for neural circuits to change. It takes a lot of metabolic energy to rearrange synaptic connections that have been firmly established over the years.[8]

3) You have to remain hopeful, despite obvious and daily drawbacks and very difficult stressful trigger-induced situations. Optimism in the face of adversity is a critical component for success. It has been found that a moderate optimistic outlook can motivate adaptive behaviors for future goals.[9] In other words, optimism can help keep you following your regime of managing the disorder despite discomfort, agitation, and pain.

4) You must firmly believe that you are normal in every sense of the word. You have a neurological disorder that creates challenges and disruptions, and while it can cause unbearable despair, it does not alter your value or worth as a human being. You have every right to a life of joy. It is through this belief that you can accept that life comes with opportunities and disadvantages for everyone. You have the fortune of knowing your disadvantage and have the opportunity to say to yourself, "I have a disorder and my life is and will be good."

5) Chances for success are optimized by early intervention. If and where possible, it is important to seek intervention when the sufferer is young and as temporally close as possible to the disorder's onset. Triggers expand and can worsen as a person ages. Through time, emotional and psychological associations with triggers—the source,

environment, and the situation—further disrupt the sufferer's well being.

Therapy

In the days when psychoanalysis was the therapy de rigueur, unresolved conflict with one's parents was considered a plausible cause of neurotic behaviors. Symptoms of "Sound-Rage" were not thought of as a consequence of neurological dysfunction. Rather, behaviors were seen as a result of aberrant relationships that imposed mental, physical, and/or sexual abuse or were seen as a result of traumatic experience. Even today, there are therapists who assume the cause of anger responses to auditory, visual, and olfactory stimuli is unresolved conflict. As a consequence of the paradigm that behaviors and thoughts are a result of unresolved feelings, the real underlying issues associated with "danger!" and "pain!" are not addressed in psychoanalytic therapy.

Declaring that the automatic behaviors that are a result of neurology are signs of neurosis creates unnecessary worry for the sufferer-patient. The pathologizing of the anger responses to triggers only serves to induce anxiety and perseveration about mental stability. Sufferers have stated that traditional psychoanalysis does not result in changes to symptom severity and intensity. Psychoanalysis clearly has its place as a viable therapeutic tool, but its appropriateness for "Sound-Rage" is limited.

Many conventional forms of talk-therapy have proven to be ineffective due to the unique nature of pain and anger in the disorder and the hard-wiring of signal firing. Psychotherapists who rely on diagnoses for treatment protocols are doomed to failure, because known disorders such as "phobia" or "social anxiety" are predicated on fear, rather than anger. It has been repeatedly expressed through testimonies that exposure therapy actually aggravates the symptoms. As discussed in earlier chapters, exposure to pain does not help one habituate to it.

Fortunately, there are therapies that can help individuals manage their symptoms, reduce trigger expansion, and eliminate associated triggers that have developed through time. There are also coping mechanisms that provide a means to avoid or block triggers. While these mechanisms are inherently limited to temporary respite, they do provide some relief from pain, anger, and frustration so that an individual can focus on the task at hand.

## Cognitive behavioral therapy (CBT)

Cognitive behavioral therapy (CBT) is a form of psychotherapy that approaches behavior and feelings as interactive with, and controlled through, thought. Therapy is a composite of teachable skills and techniques designed around an individual's unique strengths and clinical challenges. Therapist and patient work together as a team to craft specific schemes to deal with feelings and behaviors for delineated specific problems.

Therapy is problem-focused, goal-directed, and is often accompanied by homework to encourage the individual to consciously practice throughout the day as situations arise. CBT does not "cure" the sufferer of the disorder; the fundamental neurological dysfunction of "Sound-Rage" will remain unchanged. However it is an effective tool for breaking the strength of associations from one trigger to the next so that 1) new triggers do not form and take on meaning and 2) existing triggers have a less formative presence.

Neurologically speaking, trigger expansion is a *fait accompli*. Trigger expansion occurs because 1) sensory processing in the brain is multi-modal and 2) higher learning centers of the brain make learned associations. Warding off new triggers through conscious thought and learning to minimize the impact of significant triggers offers the freedom to go through life without constant vigilance and brain arousal. CBT teaches the skills and tools needed to modulate and manage a lifelong condition.

## CBT and "Sound-Rage"

An example of CBT is rehearsing self-statements intended to reframe a situation and facilitate healthy responses. In the case of "Sound-Rage," a sufferer learns to tell him/herself, "This is not real pain" or "That person is not trying to hurt me." Through intentional self-talk about the source of the trigger and telling the brain that the pain is not real, the trigger's intensity is weakened or diminished and the anger, hostility, and blame that consume the sufferer are lessened.

Framing thoughts that counteract the impact of a trigger severs underlying connections between triggers, blaming others, and feeling victimized.

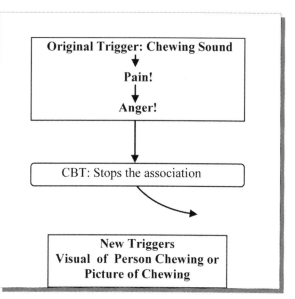

For example, when sitting in class and listening to someone's constant sniffing, the sufferer might tell him/herself, "They are not sniffing on purpose. They are not invading my space intentionally. I am perfectly safe from harm," and, "They have a cold and they are probably uncomfortable themselves. They do not mean anything by sniffing."

The brain stops the associations of feeling that personal boundaries have been crossed when engaging counteracting thoughts. The self-talk statements enhance connection through sympathy for the source (i.e., "They are probably uncomfortable themselves"), which in turn induces empathy. Empathy quells pain and quiets the brain regions of the limbic system.

In the cognitive realm: the power of empathy
Thoughts and feelings become embedded in one's belief system. In the context of pain, many beliefs that underlie the connection between trigger and discomfort are based on the assumption that the trigger's source is trying to cause harm and is acting purposefully.

Because the pain is unprovoked, it often leads the sufferer to feel victimized, although this feeling may not be a conscious one. Empathy blocks thoughts that lead to hatred and blame and relaxes an otherwise aroused mental state. As discussed in earlier chapters, empathy can serve to quiet the pain response. It is helpful to have statements that remind oneself that the source of anger is from a neurological disorder, such as, "I am normal. These feelings come from a disorder." It is also helpful to craft statements that separate the trigger from the person who is creating the trigger, such as, "That person is not really committing a crime or trying to hurt me."

In the cognitive realm: gaining control
Although sufferers of all ages may feel victimized and unable to suppress anger, children are particularly susceptible to feeling powerless. Creating new beliefs through cognition can be empowering. Self-talk that includes statements like, "I can handle this. It's okay to feel angry. This situation and my anger will pass and I'll get better at handling this every time." reinforces the individual's capability to gain control and bolster forward thinking optimism that things will improve.

Mindfulness and deep breathing to calm the aroused and angry brain
Mindfulness and relaxation exercises counter the negative impact of physiological arousal and the brain's focus on suffering. In fact, these practices relax those parts of the brain that are automatically attuned to attend to trigger stimuli. They are especially powerful when coupled with cognitive self-talk.

Mindfulness is part of an established protocol for many chronic health conditions, pain and anger management, and stress reduction. As a therapeutic technique, it teaches self-acceptance and in doing so stops the perpetuation of negative self-evaluations. It is a means of looking inward at your current state of being without becoming attached to that state of being. Mindfulness is the ability to stop and observe yourself without judgment when you are in the throes of rage from a trigger. As you become astute as a self-observer, you learn to separate yourself from the affect of pain and to diminish the anger by seeing it objectively.

Mindfulness is about being in the present moment which separates your brain from the noise of ruminating over the "who-what-when-where" of triggers. In his book *Practicing the Power of Now,* Eckhart Tolle writes, "When there is no way out, there is still always a way through. Don't let the mind use the pain to create a victim identity for yourself …. So give your complete attention to what you feel, and refrain from mentally labeling it."[10]

Deep breathing exercises play a powerful role in altering stress levels. A relatively easy form of deep breathing that can physiologically relax the body in less than a minute is conscious yawning. Brain scan studies have indicated that yawning evokes a unique neural activity in areas of the brain involved in creating feelings of empathy; it not only relaxes but it also brings the brain into a more heightened state of cognitive awareness.

<u>Avoidance Strategies: white noise generators and other blocking mechanisms</u>
White noise generators and other blocking mechanisms such as ear plugs, ear buds, and headphones are tools in the arsenal of avoiding sound triggers. They are immediate solutions to a long term problem. There is no evidence that using noise generators reduces trigger expansion or has any effect on subsequent cognitive associations. They neither empower nor enable an individual to call upon their own resources to moderate emotions and physiological changes.

Sound generators— white noise makers that are used directly at the ear—are available through audiologists. Used in concert with therapy, they are especially valuable in environments where immediate performance is required, such as test taking. Because they block sound, they literally separate the sufferer from upset because the body remains in a less aroused state. The need for the hypervigilance that transfers attention from performance on a task (any task at hand) to attention on potential triggers is reduced or eliminated.

An avoidance strategy can be preferential or necessary when you must interact in environments where triggers are prevalent and your attention to performance is mandatory. For example, students must attend school and take tests. There are times when focusing on the teacher or being relaxed and centered when taking a test requires all the emotional and psychological energy you can muster. Similarly, adults must make a living. There are times at work when you must be present: you cannot leave the board room when a vote is being taken because someone is sniffing and you cannot leave a job interview because the interviewer is chewing gum. A blocking mechanism is an effective tool that allows an individual to focus on a task at hand without succumbing to the hormonal changes accompanying the physiological arousal for flight and anger.

# Epilogue

I had hoped that if I read enough, studied enough, investigated enough, played a detective and followed every single lead, I would find the one brain part that didn't work or the one neurotransmitter that was not transmitting. I would not only figure out why the brain wasn't working right, but I would discover how it wasn't working right. And then I would be able to point to how to fix it. Most of that did not happen. I didn't find all the answers. This is what I learned:

People with this disorder are not only in pain, but they are unnecessarily suffering from worry that there is something terribly wrong with them and that they might be "crazy." There is confusion and shame that arise when reactions of anger are difficult, if not impossible, to control. "Sound-Rage," or whatever moniker is given to this disorder, is a neurological issue that has unfortunate and unforgiving symptoms. It is important for each sufferer to accept that being human means owning a unique host of physical and psychological attributes, some of which are special gifts and others difficult and relentless burdens. Like epilepsy or Parkinson's disease or Tourette disorder, "Sound-Rage" is nothing more and nothing less than a condition that one must learn to manage on a daily basis.

There is no cure. Like Tourette syndrome, the disorder is a developmental, neurological condition and like Tourette there is no magic bullet. The association between a trigger stimulus and anger is not learned, at least not for the original triggers, but is due to some fundamental shift in how the brain operates. A shrinkage in gray matter? A broken or dysfunctional neural synapse? Someday science may uncover the mechanisms by which the neural firing goes awry. Until such time, sufferers from this and other neurological disorders will be best served by finding ways to manage their symptoms and continue to strive for a life that holds joy.

Unlike most psychiatric disorders, this one is not fear-based but rather is uniquely characterized by anger without overt aggression. I conceptualize it as anger-from-pain. Pain explains many of the syndrome's mysteries: why the reaction of immediate anger leads to fleeing rather than overt aggression; why sufferers perceive the source of the triggers as acting purposely and why they create belief systems of blame; why the disorder leads to emotional isolation, feelings of vulnerability, and the need for an expanded and protected personal space.

The syndrome typically begins with one or two triggers, most likely auditory, but soon expands to include visual and olfactory stimuli. The severity of the trigger or its ability to cause extreme discomfort is laid down as an implicit memory, i.e., a memory that cannot be retrieved by the conscious mind. Daily living requires choreography of attending to tasks at hand while avoiding triggers coming from all walks of life.

How the triggers expand is a curious and complex blend of neurobiology and psychology. The brain intermingles stimuli from different sensory modalities. Visual and auditory signals get processed together. The brain, without any conscious learning, expands triggers simply because of the way information gets processed. However, triggers can and do expand through classical conditioned learning: a stimulus associated with a response is also associated with other stimuli that occur simultaneously. By way of this relationship, new stimuli are associated with a response.

Hypervigilance, common among patients of who have post traumatic stress disorder or chronic pain, becomes a way of life. Unfortunately, focused attention on triggers serves to increase the brain's overall sensitivity to the triggers.

It is simply a matter of time before triggers take on a life of their own, which is why it is critical to manage the disorder as close as possible to the time of its onset. Early management of the disorder might prevent expansion of the triggers and the associated beliefs and thoughts that accompany them. It is the associated beliefs and judgments that give us our bearings and orientation. How close we let people to us, both literally and figuratively, depends on how vulnerable we feel. If pain is random, daily, and seemingly caused by other people (or sometimes animals), we will restrict our interactions and protect our feelings. We will create stories of blame, fill our hearts with hatred or disgust, and rarely feel safe.

Through management techniques like cognitive behavior therapy, meditation, mindfulness, and coping strategies that serve to avoid or mask the triggers, we can learn to live open and trustful lives. Despite withdrawing and retreating from pain, there is always the possibility for growth, love, closeness, and hope. Having this disorder is not a death knell. It is not a guarantee of unhappiness. It is an everyday challenge that can and must be met with daily diligence of thought. It cannot be cured but it can be contained through conscious practice.

And it can be conquered, through commitment and resolve to build the organizations that research the disorder. On September 6, 2011 the New York Times had an article headlined "When a Chomp or a Slurp Is a Trigger for Outrage." This story was subsequently read and discussed a few days later when talk show host Kelly Ripa opened her "LIVE! WITH REGIS AND KELLY" show by revealing that she suffers from "Misophonia." Although it did not stir change within medical or research communities, many people with the disorder were astounded to learn that their life "quirk" was a condition shared by others. Awareness and research are attainable through the strength and viability of organizations. By establishing a non-profit association or comparable group, "Sound-Rage" sufferers, caregivers, and medical teams will find a place for dialogue, support, and targeted scientific research.

The disorder is fertile ground for scientific inquiry. It comes with a ready and willing population of subjects for whom genuine anger can easily be stimulated in the laboratory. The medical community can study entirely new possibilities for understanding and treating pain. It offers the psychological research world an entirely new arena for the study of anger without overt aggression.

I hope that this primer serves as an opening for many research endeavors to come, and contributes to building a community of support and understanding. This much we owe to our children.

# REFERENCES

## INTRODUCTION

1. Jastreboff, M. & Pawel, J. (2001, July). Components of decreased sound tolerance: hyperacusis, misophonia, phonophobia. ITHS Newsletter. Retrieved online from: http://www.tinnitus.org/home/frame/DST_NL2_PJMJ.pdf

2. Baguley, D.M. (2003). Hyperacusis. *Journal of the Royal Society of Medicine,* 96(12), 582–585.

3. Schwartz, P., Leyendecker, J., & Conlon, M. (2011). Hyperacusis and misophonia: the lesser-known siblings of tinnitus. *Minnesota Medicine,* 94(11), 42-3. Retrieved online from: http://www.medterms.com

4. Møller, R., Langguth, B., DeRidder, D., Kleinjung, T. (Eds.). (2011). *Textbook of Tinnitus.* New York: Springer.

5. Online forums in 2012. The list is not exhaustive and not all-inclusive. Quotations in the primer are taken from websites, online forums, and from personal communication. The majority of quotes were retrieved online from some of the following sites. The names of all individuals have been changed to protect privacy. Some of these forums may be temporary and may not be available after 2012.
- http://www.misophonia.info/Forum
- http://health.groups.yahoo.com/group/Soundsensitivity/
- http://www.misophonia-uk.org/
- http://www.thekitchn.com/misophonia-the-unbearable-loud-155746
- http://www.experienceproject.com/groups/Hate-Chewing-Noises/56584
- http://soundcheck.wnyc.org/2011/sep/12/mystery-misophonia/
- http://www.sodahead.com/living/does-anyone-suffer-from-misophonia-how-do-you-cope/question-946628/
- http://www.alifeofsugarandspice.com/2010/04/misophonia.html
- http://audiology.advanceweb.com/Article/Selective-Sound-Sensitivity-Syndrome.aspx
- http://www.brighthubeducation.com/student-assessment-tools/27648-sound-sensitivity-in-school-aged-children-misophonia/

- http://en.allexperts.com/q/Phobias-3097/f/Unable-tolerate-chewing-smacking.htm
- http://www.drphil.com/messageboard/topic/2703/64/
- http://bipolar.about.com/b/2012/02/06/highly-sensitive-to-noise.htm
- http://www.huffingtonpost.com/2011/09/08/misophonia-annoying-noises-disorder_n_953892.html
- http://www.post-gazette.com/stories/news/health/for-sufferers-of-misophonia-silence-is-golden-664657/
- www.chat-hyperacusis.net/
- http://www.addforums.com

6. Schröder A, Vulink, N., & Denys, D. (2013). Misophonia: diagnostic criteria for a new psychiatric disorder. *PLoS One*, 8(1). Retrieved online from: http://www.ncbi.nlm.nih.gov/pubmed/23372758

## CHAPTER 2: Stories and Testimonies from the Community

1. Barrett, L., Mesquita, B., Ochsner, K., & Gross, J. (2007). The experience of emotion. *Annual Review of Psychology,* 58, 373-403. Quote from p.376.

2. See note #3, INTRODUCTION or see reference #5, INTRODUCTION

## CHAPTER 3: All about Triggers

1. Mosby's Medical Dictionary. (9th ed.). (2012). St. Louis, MO: Mosby/Elsevier

2. Canadian Centre for Occupational Health and Safety (2012). Retrieved online from: http://www.ccohs.ca/oshanswers/phys_agents/non_auditory.html

3. Canadian Centre for Occupational Health and Safety (2012). Retrieved online from: http://www.ccohs.ca/oshanswers/phys_agents/non_auditory.html

4. Bourne, L., Jr. & Yaroush, R. (2003, February). Stress and cognition: A cognitive psychological perspective. National Aeronautics and Space Administration, Grant Number NAG2-1561. Retrieved online from:

http://humansystems.arc.nasa.gov/eas/download/non_EAS/Stress_and_Co
gnition.pdf

5. See note #3, INTRODUCTION or see reference #5, INTRODUCTION.


CHAPTER 4: Do I Have this Syndrome?

1. See note #3, INTRODUCTION or see reference #5, INTRODUCTION.


CHAPTER 5: What's the Diagnosis?

1-4. See note #3, INTRODUCTION or see reference #5,
INTRODUCTION.

5. Walkup, J. (2009, June). Tourette syndrome research: past, present and
future. The big picture, where neurobiology meets environment. Fifth
International Scientific Symposium on Tourette Syndrome, New York.
Retrieved online from: http://www.tsa-
usa.org/aResearch/TSA5thSciSympos_LS_ed_rev9_4_09.pdf

6. Haber, S. (2009, June). Neural circuits and TS: integrative networks
across basal ganglia circuits.      Fifth International Scientific Symposium
on Tourette Syndrome, New York. Retrieved online from: http://www.tsa-
usa.org/aResearch/TSA5thSciSympos_LS_ed_rev9_4_09.pdf

7. Bauer, A. & Shea, T. (1984). Tourette syndrome: a review and
educational implications. *Journal of Autism and Developmental Disorders*,
14(1).

8. Retrieved online : http://www.ocduk.org/tourette-syndrome-history

9. Evans, D. L., Foa, E.B., Gur, R., Hendin, H., O'Brien, C., Seligman, M.,
Walsh, B., William T., & Ruane, J. (Eds.). (2005). *Treating and
Preventing Adolescent Mental Health Disorders.* New York, NY: Oxford
University Press.

10. See note #3, INTRODUCTION or see reference #5,
INTRODUCTION.

11. American Psychiatric Association. (2000). *Diagnostic and statistical
manual of mental disorders* (4th ed.). Washington, DC.

12. Retrieved online from:
http://today.msnbc.msn.com/id/44438402/ns/today-today_health/t/when-annoying-sounds-spark-major-rage/#.UHMrF67orf0.

13. Retrieved online from: http://www.ntis.gov/pdf/ptsdbasicstext.pdf

14. American Psychiatric Association. (2011). Let's talk facts about what is posttraumatic stress disorder. Retrieved online from: www.healthyminds.org

15. Kessler, R., Sonnega, A., Bromet, E., Hughes, M, & Nelson, C. (1995). Posttraumatic stress disorder in the national comorbidity survey. *Arch Gen Psychiatry,* 52(12), 1048-1060.

16. Helzer, J., Robins, L., & McEvoy, L. (1987). Post-traumatic stress disorder in the general population. *New England Journal of Medicine,* 317, 1630–4.

17. Dr. Phil show, "Am I the only one?" Retrieved online from:
http://drphil.com/slideshows/slideshow/5518/?id=5518&slide=1&showID=1374&preview=&versionID=

18. See note #3, INTRODUCTION or see reference #5, INTRODUCTION.

19. Miller, J.L. & Fuller, D. (2006). *Sensational kids: hope and help for children with sensory processing Disorder.* New York, NY: Penguin Group

20. Kivi, R. (2011). The similarities between misophonia and sensory processing disorder: is there a link? Retrieved online from: http://www.healthguideinfo.com/neurological-disorders/p100641/

21. Pfeiffer, B. & Kinnealey, M. (2003). Treatment of sensory defensiveness in adults. *Occupational Therapy International,* 10(3), 175-184.

22. Heller, S. (2003). *Too Loud, Too Bright, Too Fast, Too Tight: What to do if you are sensory defensive in an overstimulating world.* New York, NY: Quill.

CHAPTER 6: The Brain: Overview

1. Hromádka, T., DeWeese, M., & Zador, A. (2012, January). Sparse representation of sounds in the unanesthetized auditory cortex. Public Library of Science: Biology. Retrieved online from: http://www.plosbiology.org/article/info:doi/10.1371/journal.pbio.0060016

2. See note #3, INTRODUCTION or see reference #5, INTRODUCTION

3. King A., & Schnupp, J. W.H. (2007, April). The auditory cortex. *Current Biology,* 17(7).

4. Gordon, E., Liddell, B., Brown, K., Bryant, R., & Clark, C.R. (2007). Integrating objective gene-brain-behavior markers of psychiatric disorders. *Journal of Integrative Neuroscience*, 6(1), 1–34.

5. Gordon, E., Liddell, B., Brown, K., Bryant, R., & Clark, C.R. (2007). Integrating objective gene-brain-behavior markers of psychiatric disorders. *Journal of Integrative Neuroscience*, 6(1), 1–34.

6. Gordon, E., Liddell, B., Brown, K., Bryant, R., & Clark, C.R. (2007). Integrating objective gene-brain-behavior markers of psychiatric disorders. *Journal of Integrative Neuroscience*, 6(1), 1–34.

7. Ledoux, J. (1996). *The Emotional Brain.* New York, NY: Simon and Schuster. Quote from p. 69.

8 . Ledoux, J. (1996). *The Emotional Brain.* New York, NY: Simon and Schuster.

9. Ledoux, J. (1996). *The Emotional Brain.* New York, NY: Simon and Schuster. Quote from p. 69.

10. Ledoux, J. (1996). *The Emotional Brain.* New York, NY: Simon and Schuster.


CHAPTER 7: The Trigger Brain

1. Salzman, D. & Fusil, S. (2010). Emotion, cognition, and mental state representation in amygdala and prefrontal cortex. *Annual Review of Neuroscience*, 33,173-202.

2. Gruters, K. & Groh, J. (2012). Sounds and beyond: multisensory and other non-auditory signals in the inferior colliculus. *Frontiers in Neural Circuits*, 6, 96.

3. Salzman, D. & Fusil, S. (2010). Emotion, cognition, and mental state representation in amygdala and prefrontal cortex. *Annual Review of Neuroscience*, 33, 173-202.

4. Salzman, D. & Fusil, S. (2010). Emotion, cognition, and mental state representation in amygdala and prefrontal cortex. *Annual Review of Neuroscience*, 33, 173-202.

5. Gruters, K. and Groh, J. (2012). Sounds and beyond: multisensory and other non-auditory signals in the inferior colliculus. *Frontiers in Neural Circuits,* 6, 96.

6. Graeff, F. (1994). Neuroanatomy and neurotransmitter regulation of defensive behaviors and related emotions in mammals. *Brazilian Journal of Medical and Biological Research*, 27(4), 811-29.

7. Barbas, H., Zikopoulos, B., & Timbie, C. (2010, August). Sensory pathways and emotional context for action in primate prefrontal cortex. *Biological Psychiatry,* 68(11). Retrieved online from: http://cns-pc62.bu.edu/cn730/spring-2011/PDF/W7%20Barbas%20et%20al%20%282010%29.pdf

8. Pessoa, L. & Adolphs, R. (2010, November). Emotion processing and the amygdala: from a 'low road' to 'many roads' of evaluating biological significance. *Nature Reviews Neuroscience*, 11(11), 773–783.

9. Pessoa, L. & Adolphs, R. (2010, November). Emotion processing and the amygdala: from a 'low road' to 'many roads' of evaluating biological significance. *Nature Reviews Neuroscience*, 11(11), 773–783.

10. Neuroscience Online Textbook Byrne, J. (ed.) (2012). Retrieved online from: http://neuroscience.uth.tmc.edu/s4/chapter06.html

11. Anders, S., Eippert, F., Weiskopf, N. & Veit, R. (2008). The human amygdala is sensitive to the valence of pictures and sounds irrespective of arousal: an fMRI study. *Social Cognitive and Affective Neuroscience*, 3(3):233-243. Retrieved online from: http://scan.oxfordjournals.org/content/3/3/233.short

12. Zald D.H., Pardo J.V. (2002). The neural correlates of aversive auditory stimulation. *Neuroimage,* 16,746 –753.

13. Höistad, M., & Barbas, H. (2008, April). Sequence of information processing for emotions through pathways linking temporal and insular cortices with the amygdala. *Neuroimage,* 40(3), 1016–1033.

14. Hendler T., Rotshtein, P., Yeshurun,Y., Weizmann,T., Kahn,I., Ben-Bashat,D., Malach,R., & Bleich,A. (2003, July). Sensing the invisible: differential sensitivity of visual cortex and amygdala to traumatic context. *Neuroimage,* 19(3), 587-600.

15. Canli, T., Zhao, Z., Brewer, J., Gabrieli, J.D., & Cahill, L. (2000, October 1). Event-related activation in the human amygdala associates with later memory for individual emotional experience. *Journal of Neuroscience,* (19), RC99.

16. Van Marle, H.J., Hermans, E.J., Qin, S., & Fernández, G.(2010). Enhanced resting-state connectivity of amygdala in the immediate aftermath of acute psychological stress. *Neuroimage,* 53(1), 348-54.

17. Hromádka, T., DeWeese, M. & Zador, A. (2008, January 29). Sparse representation of sounds in the unanesthetized auditory cortex. *PLoS Biol,* 6(1): e16. Retrieved online from: http://www.plosbiology.org/article/info:doi/10.1371/journal.pbio.0060016

18. Kilian-Hütten, N., Valente, G., Vroomen, J., & Formisano, E. (2011, Feb 2). Auditory cortex encodes the perceptual interpretation of ambiguous sound. *Journal of Neuroscience,* 31(5), 1715-20.

19. Salzman, D. & Fusil, S. (2010). Emotion, cognition, and mental state representation in amygdala and prefrontal cortex. *Annual Review of Neuroscience,* 33,173-202.

20. Salzman, D. & Fusil, S. (2010). Emotion, cognition, and mental state representation in amygdala and prefrontal cortex. *Annual Review of Neuroscience,* 33,173-202.

21. Sander, D., Grandjean, D., Pourtois, G., Schwartz, S., Seghier, M., Scherer, K. & Vuilleumier, P. (2005). Emotion and attention interactions in social cognition: brain regions involved in processing anger prosody. *NeuroImage,* 28, 848–858.

22. Frey, S., Kostopoulos, P., & Petrides, M. (2003, September).Orbitofrontal involvement in the processing of unpleasant auditory information. *European Journal of Neuroscience*, 12(10), 3709–3712.

23. Medford, N. & Critchley, H. (2010, June). Conjoint activity of anterior insular and anterior cingulate cortex: awareness and response. *Brain Structure and Function*, 214(5-6), 535–549. Retrieved online from: http://www.ncbi.nlm.nih.gov/pmc/articles/PMC2886906/

CHAPTER 8: Brain Circuitry and Triggers

1. LeDoux, J. (2002). *Synaptic self: how our brains become who we are.* New York, NY: Penguin Group. Quote from p.164.

2. Salzman, D. & Fusil, S. (2010). Emotion, cognition, and mental state representation in amygdala and prefrontal cortex. *Annual Review of Neuroscience*, 33, 173-202.

3. Barrett, L., Mesquita, B., Ochsner, K., & Gross, J. (2007). The Experience of emotion. *Annual Rev. Psychology*, 58, 373-403. Retrieved online from: http://dept.psych.columbia.edu/~kochsner/pdf/Barrett_AR_2006.pdf

4. Kumar, S. von Kriegstein, K., Friston, K. & Griffiths, T. (2012, October). Features versus feelings: dissociable representations of the acoustic features and valence of aversive sounds. *Journal of Neuroscience*, 32(41), 14184 –14192.

5. LeDoux, J. (2002). *Synaptic self: how our brains become who we are.* New York, NY: Penguin Group. Quote from p.122.

6. Adolphs, R. (2002, April). Neural systems for recognizing emotion. *Current Opinion in Neurobiology*, 12(2), 169-77.

7. King A. & Schnupp, J. (2007). The auditory cortex. *Current Biology*, 17(7), 236-239.

8. Pessoa, L. & Adolphs, R. (Nov 2010). Emotion processing and the amygdala: from a 'low road' to 'many roads' of evaluating biological significance. *Nature Reviews Neuroscience*, 11(11), 773–783.

9. Barbas, H., Zikopoulos, B., & Timbie, C. (2010, August). Sensory pathways and emotional context for action in primate prefrontal cortex. *Biological Psychiatry*, 68(11). Retrieved online from: http://cns-pc62.bu.edu/cn730/spring-2011/PDF/W7%20Barbas%20et%20al%20%282010%29.pdf.

10. Mutschler, I., Wieckhorst, B., Kowalevski, S., Derix, J., Wentlandt, J., Schulze-Bonhage, A. & Ball, T. (2009, June) Functional organization of the human anterior insular cortex. *Neuroscience Letters*, 457(2), 66–70.

11. Barbas, H., Zikopoulos, B., & Timbie, C. (2010, August). Sensory pathways and emotional context for action in primate prefrontal cortex. *Biological Psychiatry*, 68(11). Retrieved online from:    http://cns-pc62.bu.edu/cn730/spring-2011/PDF/W7%20Barbas%20et%20al%20%2820 10%29.pdf.

12. Paulus, M & Stein, M. (2006, August). An insular view of anxiety. *Biological Psychiatry*, 60(4):383-7.

13. Medford, N. & Critchley, H. (2010, June).  Conjoint activity of anterior insular and anterior cingulate cortex: awareness and response. *Brain Structure and Function*, 214(5-6), 535–549. Retrieved online from: http://www.ncbi.nlm.nih.gov/pmc/articles/PMC2886906/

14. Sander, D., Grandjean, D., Pourtois, G., Schwartz, S., Seghier, M., Scherer, K. & Vuilleumier, P. (2005). Emotion and attention interactions in social cognition: brain regions involved in processing anger prosody. *NeuroImage*, 28, 848 – 858.

15. Adolphs, R. (2002, April). Neural systems for recognizing emotion. *Current Opinion in Neurobiology*, 12(2):169-77.

16. Croy, I., Olgun S., & Joraschky, P. (2011, December). Basic emotions elicited by odors and pictures. *Emotion*.11(6), 1331-5.

17. Retrieved online (2012) from: www.wikipedia.com

18. Zald, D., & Pardo, J. (1997, April). Emotion, olfaction, and the human amygdala: amygdala activation during aversive olfactory stimulation. *Proceedings of the National Academy of Sciences*, 94(8), 4119–4124.

19. Krusemark, E., & Li, W. (2102, March). Enhanced olfactory sensory perception of threat in anxiety: an event-related fMRI study. *Chemosensory Perception*, 5(1), 37–45.

20. Seubert, J., Kellermann, T., Loughead, J., Boers, F., Brensinger, C., Schneider F, & Habel, U. (2010, July). Processing of disgusted faces is facilitated by odor primes: a functional MRI study. *NeuroImage*, 53(2), 746-56.

21. Suzuki A. (2010, November). Insula and disgust. *Rinsho Shinkeigaku*, 50(11), 1000-2.

22. Troiani, V., Price, E., & Schultz, R. (2012, October 9). Unseen fearful faces promote amygdala guidance of attention. *Social Cognitive and Affective Neuroscience*. Retrieved online from: http://scan.oxfordjournals.org/content/early/2012/10/25/scan.nss116.abstract

CHAPTER 9: The Brain and Multi-Sensory Processing

1. King, A. (2006). Auditory Neuroscience: Activating the Cortex without Sound. *Current Biology*, 16(11).

2. Schroeder, C. & Foxe, J. (2005). Multisensory contributions to low-level, 'unisensory' processing. *Current Opinion in Neurobiology*, 15, 454–458.

3. Fu, K., Johnston, T., Shah, A., Arnold, L., Smiley, J., Hackett, T., Garraghty, E. & Schroeder, C. (2003, August 20). Auditory cortical neurons respond to somatosensory stimulation. *The Journal of Neuroscience*, 23(20), 7510–7515.

4. Molholm, S., Ritter, W., Javitt, D., & Foxe, J. (2004, April). Multisensory visual–auditory object recognition in humans: a high-density electrical mapping study. *Cerebral Cortex*, 14, 452–465. Retrieved online from: http://cercor.oxfordjournals.org/

5. Murray, M., Foxe, J. & Wylie, G. (2005, August). The brain uses single-trial multisensory memories to discriminate without awareness. *NeuroImage*, 27(2), 473–478.

6. Rosenblum, L.D. (2008). Speech perception as a multimodal phenomenon. *Current Directions in Psychological Science*, 17, 405-409.

CHAPTER 10: A Developmental Disorder: What Can Sudden Onset Tell Us?

1. Palubinsky, A.M., Martin, J.A, & McLaughlin, B. (2012). The role of central nervous system development in late-onset neurodegenerative disorders. *Developmental Neuroscience, 34*(2-3), 129-139.

2. Personal communication, Anthony Zador, MD, PhD. (2012, September) Email correspondence. Cold Spring Harbor Laboratory, Cold Spring Harbor, NY.

3. LeDoux, J. (2002). *Synaptic self: how our brains become who we are.* New York, NY: Penguin Group.

4. See note #3, INTRODUCTION or see reference #5, INTRODUCTION.

5. Toga, A., Thompson, P., & Sowell, E. (2006, March). Mapping brain maturation. *Trends in Neuroscience*, 29(3), 148–159.

6. Toga, A., Thompson, P., & Sowell, E. (2006, March). Mapping brain maturation. *Trends in Neuroscience*, 29(3), 148–159.

7. Konrad, K. & Eickhoff, S. (2010, June). Is the ADHD brain wired differently? A review on structural and functional connectivity in attention deficit hyperactivity disorder. Special Issue: challenges and methods in developmental neuroimaging. *Human Brain Mapping*, 31(6), 904–916 Retrieved online from: http://onlinelibrary.wiley.com/doi/10.1002/hbm.21058/full

8. Konrad, K. & Eickhoff, S. (2010, June). Is the ADHD brain wired differently? A review on structural and functional connectivity in attention deficit hyperactivity disorder. Special Issue: challenges and methods in developmental neuroimaging. *Human Brain Mapping*, 31(6), 904–916. Retrieved online from: http://onlinelibrary.wiley.com/doi/10.1002/hbm.21058/full.

9. Hatton , S., Lagopoulos, J., Hermens, D., Naismith, S., Bennett, M. & Hickie, I. (2012). Correlating anterior insula gray matter volume changes in young people with clinical and neurocognitive outcomes: an MRI study. *BMC Psychiatry,* 12(45). Retrieved online from: http://www.biomedcentral.com/1471-244X/12/45#sec4

10. Medford, N. & Critchley, H. (2010, June). Conjoint activity of anterior insular and anterior cingulate cortex: awareness and response. *Brain*

*Structure and Function*, 214(5-6), 535–549. Retrieved online from: http://www.ncbi.nlm.nih.gov/pmc/articles/PMC2886906/


CHAPTER 11: Emotions Overview

1. Loewenstein, G. & Lerner, J. (2009). The role of affect in decision making. In Davidson, R., Scherer, K., & Goldsmith, H. (Eds.). *Handbook of Affective Sciences*. New York, NY: Oxford University Press.

2. Izard, C. (2009). Emotion theory and research: highlights, unanswered questions, and emerging issues. *The Annual Review of Psychology*, 60, 1–25. Retrieved online from: http://www.psych.annualreviews.org

3. Vingerhoets, J. (Ed.). (1997). The psychological context of crying: towards a model of adult crying. In *The (non)expression of emotions in health and disease*. Netherlands: Tilburg University Press. Retrieved online from: http://arno.uvt.nl/show.cgi?fid=48635

CHAPTER 12: "Sound-Rage" and Pain

1. Stemmler, G. (2010). Somatovisceral activation during anger. In Potegal, M., Stemmler, G. & Spielberger, C. (Eds.). *International Handbook of Anger*. Springer Press.

2. Cross, S.A. (1994). Pathophysiology of pain. *Journal of the Mayo Clinic*, 69(4), 3 75-383

3. Retrieved online: http://www.iasp-pain.org/Content/NavigationMenu/GeneralResourceLinks/PainDefinitions/default.htm#Pain

4. See note #3, INTRODUCTION or see reference #5, INTRODUCTION.

5. Derbyshire, S., Whalley, M., Stenger, V. & Oakley, D. (2004). Cerebral activation during hypnotically induced and imagined pain. *NeuroImage*, 23, 392 –401

6. Moskowitz, M. & Fishman, S. (2006). The Neurobiological and therapeutic intersection of pain and affective disorders. *Focus, the Journal of Life Long Learning in Psychiatry*, IV(4). Retrieved online from: http://focus.psychiatryonline.org/data/Journals/FOCUS/2645/465.pdf

7. Treede, R.D., Kenshalo, D.R, Gracely, R.H. & Jones, A.K. (1999, February). The cortical representation of pain. *Pain*, 79(2-3), 105-11.

8. Duquette, M., Roy,M., Leporé, F., Peretz, I., & Rainville, P. (2007, February). Cerebral mechanisms involved in the interaction between pain and emotion. *Review of Neurology (Paris)*, 163(2), 169-79.

9. Bruehl, S., Burns, J., Chung, O., & Chont, M. (2009, March) Pain-related effects of trait anger expression: neural substrates and the role of endogenous opioid mechanisms. *Neuroscience Biobehavior Review*, 33(3), 475–491.

10. Medford, N. & Critchley, H. (2010, June). Conjoint activity of anterior insular and anterior cingulate cortex: awareness and response. *Brain Structure and Function*, 214(5-6), 535–549. Retrieved online from: http://www.ncbi.nlm.nih.gov/pmc/articles/PMC2886906/

11. Eccleston, C. & Crombez, G. (1999, May). Pain demands attention: a cognitive–affective model of the interruptive function of pain. *Psychological Bulletin*, 125(3), 356–366.

12. Bruehl, S., Burns, J., Chung, O., & Chont, M. (2009, March) Pain-related effects of trait anger expression: neural substrates and the role of endogenous opioid mechanisms. *Neuroscience Biobehavior Review*, 33(3), 475–491.

13. Eccleston, C. & Crombez, G. (1999, May). Pain demands attention: a cognitive–affective model of the interruptive function of pain. *Psychological Bulletin*, 125(3), 356–366.

14. Hofbauer, R. Rainville, P., Duncan, G.H., & Bushnell, M.C. (2001). Cortical representation of the sensory dimension of pain. *Journal of Neurophysiology*, 86, 402-411. Retrieved online from: http://jn.physiology.org/content/86/1/402.full

15-19. See note #3, INTRODUCTION or see reference #5, INTRODUCTION.

20. Tanner, R., Ferraro, R., Chartrand, T., & Bettman, J. (2008). Of chameleons and consumption: The impact of mimicry on choice and preferences. *Journal of Consumer Research*, 34. Retrieved online from: https://faculty.fuqua.duke.edu/~jrb12/bio/Jim/mimic_final.pdf

21. Iacoboni, M. (2009, January). Imitation, empathy, and mirror neurons. *Annual Review of Psychology*, 60, 653-670.

22. Singer, T., Seymour, B., O'Doherty, J., Kaube, H., Raymond J. Dolan, R. & Frith, C. (2004, February). Empathy for pain involves the affective but not sensory components of pain. *Science, 33,* 1157-1162.

CHAPTER 13: Anger and Disgust

1-2. See note #3, INTRODUCTION or see reference #5, INTRODUCTION.

3. Matsumoto, D., Hwang, H., & Frank, M. (2012, January). The role of emotion in predicting violence. Department of FBI Law Enforcement Bulletin. Federal Bureau of Investigation, Washington, D.C

4. Bruehl, S., Burns, J., Chung, O., & Chont, M. (2009, March) Pain-related effects of trait anger expression: neural substrates and the role of endogenous opioid mechanisms. *Neuroscience Biobehavior Review,* 33(3), 475–491.

5. Izard, C. (2009). Emotion theory and research: highlights, unanswered questions, and emerging issues. *The Annual Review of Psychology,* 60,1–25. Retrieved online from: http://www.psych.annualreviews.org

6. Novaco, R. (2010). Anger and Psychopathology. In Potegal, M., Stemmler, G. & Spielberger, C. (Eds.). *International Handbook of Anger.* Springer Press.

7. McLaren, K. (2010). The language of emotions: what your feelings are trying to tell you. Boulder, CO: Sounds True Press.

8. Novaco, R. (2010). Anger and Psychopathology. In Potegal, M., Stemmler, G. & Spielberger, C. (Eds.). *International Handbook of Anger.* Springer Press.

9. McLaren, K. (2010). *The language of emotions: what your feelings are trying to tell you.* Boulder, CO: Sounds True Press.

10. Fernandez, E & Turk, D. (1995). The scope and significance of anger in the experience of chronic pain. Taken from: Berkowitz, L. Affect, aggression and antisocial behavior. In Davidson, R., Scherer, K., & Goldsmith, H. (Eds.). *Handbook of Affective Sciences.* New York, NY: Oxford University Press.

11. Bruehl, S., Burns, J., Chung, O., & Chont, M. (2009, March) Pain-related effects of trait anger expression: neural substrates and the role of endogenous opioid mechanisms. *Neuroscience Biobehavior Review*, 33(3), 475–491.

12. Siegel, A., Bhatt, S., Bhatt, R. & Zalcman, S. (2007, June). The Neurobiological bases for development of pharmacological treatments of aggressive disorders. *Current Neuropharmacology*, 5(2), 135–147.

13-16. See note #3, INTRODUCTION or see reference #5, INTRODUCTION.

17. Ahmed, A., Kingston, D., DiGiuseppe, R., Bradford, J., &. Seto, M. (2102). Developing a clinical typology of dysfunctional anger. *Journal of Affective Disorders,* 136, 139–148.

18. Berkowitz, L. (2009). Affect, aggression and antisocial behavior. (2009). In Davidson, R., Scherer, K., & Goldsmith, H. (Eds.). *Handbook of Affective Sciences*. New York, NY:Oxford University Press.

19. Mauss, I., Cook, C. & Gross, J. (2007). Automatic emotion regulation during anger provocation. *Journal of Experimental Social Psychology*, 43,698–711.

20-21. See note #3, INTRODUCTION or see reference #5, INTRODUCTION.

22. Haidt, J. (2009). The moral emotions. In Davidson, R., Scherer, K., & Goldsmith, H. (Eds.). *Handbook of Affective Sciences*. New York, NY:Oxford University Press.

23. Amato, E. (1998, January). Mystery of disgust. *Psychology Today*. Retrieved online from: http://www.psychologytoday.com/articles/200909/mystery-disgust

CHAPTER14:  Hypervigilance and  Attention to Danger

1-4. See note #3, INTRODUCTION or see reference #5, INTRODUCTION.

5. Pourtois G. & Vuilleumier P. (2006). Dynamics of emotional effects on spatial attention in the human visual cortex. *Prog Brain Res.*156, 67-91.

6. Hollins, M., Harper, D., Gallagher, S., Owings, E., Lim, P., Miller, V., Siddiqi, M. & Maixner, W. (2009, February). Perceived intensity and unpleasantness of cutaneous and auditory stimuli: an evaluation of the generalized hypervigilance hypothesis. *Pain,* 141(3), 215–221.

7. Surguladze, S. Brammer, M.J., Young, A.W., Andrew, C., Travis, M.J., Williams, S.C. & Phillips, M.L. (2003). A preferential increase in the extrastriate response to signals of danger. *NeuroImage.* 19, 1317–1328.

8. King, A. (2006). Auditory Neuroscience: Activating the Cortex without Sound. *Current Biology,* 16(11).

CHAPTER 15: Cognition: How the Brain Thinks about Triggers

1. Mesulam, M.M. (1998, June). From sensation to cognition. *Brain.* 121 (Pt 6), 1013-52. Retrieved online from: http://www.ncbi.nlm.nih.gov/pubmed/9648540

2. See note #3, INTRODUCTION or see reference #5, INTRODUCTION.

3. Larsen, J., Berntson, G., Poehlmann, K., Ito, T. & Cacioppo, J (2006). The psychophysiology of emotion. Draft of a chapter to appear in R. Lewis, J. M. Haviland-Jones, & L. F. Barrett (Eds.). *The handbook of emotions* (third edition). New York, NY: Guilford Press.

4. Barrett, L., Mesquita, B., Ochsner, K., & Gross, J. (2007). The experience of emotion. *Annual Review of Psychology,* 58,373–403.

5. Izard, C. (2009). Emotion theory and research: highlights, unanswered questions, and emerging issues. *The Annual Review of Psychology,* 60,1–25. Retrieved online from: http://www.psych.annualreviews.org

6. See note #3, INTRODUCTION or see reference #5, INTRODUCTION.

7. Killgore, W. & Yurgelun-Todd, D.A. (2007). Unconscious processing of facial affect in children and adolescents. *Social Neuroscience,* 2, 28–47.

8. Darwin, C. (1872). *The Expression of the Emotions in man and animals (1ˢᵗ Edition).* London: John Murray.

9. Mclaren, K. *The Language of Emotion.* (2010). Boulder CO:Sounds True Press

10. See note #3, INTRODUCTION or see reference #5, INTRODUCTION.

11. Sternberg, R. (2003). A duplex theory of hate: development and application to terrorism, massacres, and genocide. *Review of General Psychology,* 7(3), 299-328.

CHAPTER 16: Trigger Expansion

1. Begley, S. (2008). *Train your mind, change your brain. How a new science reveals our extraordinary potential to transform ourselves.* New York: Ballantine Books.

2. Hollins, M., Harper, D., Gallagher, S., Owings, E., Lim, P., Miller, V., Siddiqi, M. & Maixner, W. (2009, February). Perceived intensity and unpleasantness of cutaneous and auditory stimuli: an evaluation of the generalized hypervigilance hypothesis. *Pain,* 141(3), 215–221.

3. Senkowski, D., Schneider,T., Foxe, J., & Engel, A. (2008). Crossmodal binding through neural coherence: implications for multisensory processing. *Trends in Neurosciences,* 31(8).

4. Schroeder, C. & Foxe, J. (2005). Multisensory contributions to low-level, 'unisensory' processing. *Current Opinion in Neurobiology,* 15, 454–458.

5. Murray, M., Foxe, J. & Wylie, G.(2005, August). The brain uses single-trial multisensory memories to discriminate without awareness. *NeuroImage,* 27, 473-8.

6. Shams, L., Wozny, D., Kim, R. & Seitz, A. (2011). Influences of multisensory experience on subsequent unisensory processing. *Frontiers in Psychology,* 2, 264. Retrieved online from: http://www.ncbi.nlm.nih.gov/pmc/articl6. es/PMC3198541/

7. Lewis, J., Wightman, F., Brefczynski, B. , Raymond, E., Phinney, R., Binder, J. & DeYoel,E. (2004, September). Human brain regions involved in recognizing environmental sounds. *Cerebral Cortex,*14, 1008–1021. Retrieved online from: http://www.hsc.wvu.edu/wvucn/MediaLibraries/WVUCN/Media/People/Lewis/pdfs/Lewis_etal_2004_CerebCtx.pdf

8. Shams, L., Wozny, D., Kim, R. & Seitz, A. (2011). Influences of multisensory experience on subsequent unisensory processing. *Frontiers in Psychology*, 2, 264.

CHAPTER 17: Therapies

1-7. See note #3, INTRODUCTION or see reference #5, INTRODUCTION.

8. Newberg, A. & Waldman, M. (2009). *How God changes your brain. Breakthrough findings from a leading neuroscientist.* New York, NY: Ballantine Books.

9. Sharot, T., Riccardi A., Raio, C. & , Phelps, E. (2007). Neural mechanisms mediating optimism bias. *Nature,* 450(7166), 102-5. Retrieved online from: http://www.psych.nyu.edu/phelpslab/new/papers/07_Nature_V449.pdf

10. Tolle, E. (1999). *Practicing the power of now. Essential teachings, meditations and exercises from the power of now.* Novato, CA: New World Library.

# NOTES

## INTRODUCTION

1. Wakefield, J. C. (1992). The concept of mental disorder. On the boundary between biological facts and social values. *Am Psychol*. 47(3), 373-88. New York, NY

"Although the concept of mental disorder is fundamental to theory and practice in the mental health field, no agreed on and adequate analysis of this concept currently exists. I argue that a disorder is a harmful dysfunction, wherein harmful is a value term based on social norms, and dysfunction is a scientific term referring to the failure of a mental mechanism to perform a natural function for which it was designed by evolution. Thus, the concept of disorder combines value and scientific components."

2. Møller, R., Langguth, B., DeRidder, D., Kleinjung, T. (Eds.). (2011). *Textbook of Tinnitus*. New York:Springer

"The word misophonia has yet to enter widespread usage and is not a recognized term in many healthcare databases such as Medline. It does, however, add a useful definition to the terminology of reduced loudness tolerance, and its usage should probably be encouraged."

3. Sampling of online forums in 2012. The list is not exhaustive and not all-inclusive. Quotations are taken from public websites, online forums, and from personal communication. The majority of quotes were retrieved from some of the following sites. Some of these forums and listserves are temporary and may not be available at time of printing (2013). The names of all individuals have been changed to protect privacy.

- http://www.misophonia.info/Forum
- http://health.groups.yahoo.com/group/Soundsensitivity/
- http://www.misophonia-uk.org/
- http://www.thekitchn.com/misophonia-the-unbearable-loud-155746
- http://www.experienceproject.com/groups/Hate-Chewing-Noises/56584
- http://soundcheck.wnyc.org/2011/sep/12/mystery-misophonia/
- http://www.sodahead.com/living/does-anyone-suffer-from-misophonia-how-do-you-cope/question-946628/

- http://www.alifeofsugarandspice.com/2010/04/misophonia.html
- http://audiology.advanceweb.com/Article/Selective-Sound-Sensitivity-Syndrome.aspx
- http://www.brighthubeducation.com/student-assessment-tools/27648-sound-sensitivity-in-school-aged-children-misophonia/
- http://en.allexperts.com/q/Phobias-3097/f/Unable-tolerate-chewing-smacking.htm
- http://www.drphil.com/messageboard/topic/2703/64/
- http://bipolar.about.com/b/2012/02/06/highly-sensitive-to-noise.htm
- http://www.huffingtonpost.com/2011/09/08/misophonia-annoying-noises-disorder_n_953892.html
- http://www.post-gazette.com/stories/news/health/for-sufferers-of-misophonia-silence-is-golden-664657/
- www.chat-hyperacusis.net/
- http://www.addforums.com

4. Merriam-Webster defines empirical evidence as "originating in or based on observation or experiment." In the case of "Sound-Rage," evidence is derived from observation and inquiry. To date, there are no experimentally designed studies on the disorder.

## CHAPTER 3: All about Triggers

1. Schröder A, Vulink, N., & Denys, D. (2013). Misophonia: diagnostic criteria for a new psychiatric disorder. PLoS One. 8(1). Retrieved online from: http://www.ncbi.nlm.nih.gov/pubmed/23372758

Forty two Dutch patients were clinically assessed using a standard psychiatric interview by five psychiatrists experienced in obsessive-compulsive spectrum disorders. Adapting the Yale-Brown Obsessive-Compulsive Scale (Y-BOCS), patients were asked about the (1) time they spent on misophonia; (2) interference with social functioning; (3) level of anger; (4) resistance against the impulse; (5) control they had over their thoughts and anger; and (6) time they spent avoiding misophonic situations. Scores from 0–4 are considered subclinical misophonic symptoms, 5–9 mild, 10–14 moderate, 15–19 severe, 20–24 extreme. Five patients were randomly selected to perform a standard hearing test; no significant audiological distortion was found and further testing was therefore omitted.

Findings:
- Mean age of onset was 13 years (range 2–38).

- In all 42 patients we found a remarkably similar pattern of symptoms
- Triggering stimuli were all sounds produced by humans. Animal or other sounds usually did not cause distress, nor did sounds made by the patients themselves.
- Symptoms in 34 patients (81%) were triggered by eating-related sounds like lip smacking.
- 27 patients (64.3%) mentioned (loud) breathing or nose sounds as provocative.
- 25 patients (59.5%) could not tolerate the sound of typing on a keyboard or pen clicking sounds.
- The stimuli were initially auditory and sometimes expanded to visual stimuli, with the image directly related to the triggering sound (e.g. watching someone else eat also caused arousal).
- Five patients (11.9%) reported a misophonia-like reaction when confronted with certain repetitive visual movements made by another person such as leg rocking (in analogy to misophonia this can be named *misokinesia*, meaning hatred of movement).
- Exposure to the misophonic stimulus provoked an immediate aversive physical reaction, starting with irritation (59.5%) or disgust (40.5%) that instantaneously became anger.
- 12 patients (28.6%) described getting verbally aggressive on occasions.
- Seven patients (16.7%) admitted physical aggression directed towards objects.
- Five patients (11.9%) hit an (ex-) partner once.
- Anxiety was explicitly not experienced.
- The intensity of the anger with rare but potential aggressive outbursts initiated a profound feeling of loss of self-control.
- Patients had insight and perceived their aggressive reaction as excessive and unreasonable and estimated the loss of self-control as morally unacceptable.
- All patients actively avoided the misophonic stimuli by avoiding social situations, wearing headsets or producing anti-sounds that resulted in marginal social contacts.
- Patients experienced daily stress or discomfort by anticipating an unexpected encounter with misophonic stimuli. The severity of symptoms on the concept A-MISO-S was severe (15.1 out of 24. Range: 9–22).
- Three patients (7.1%) were diagnosed with a co-morbid mood disorder.

- Depressive and anxiety symptoms and overall psychoneuroticism were reported higher than in the general population (HAM-D score: mean 7.3, range 0–22; HAM-A: mean 11.2, range 0–31; SCL90: mean 156.7, range 93–294).
- Their personality showed traits of obsessive-compulsive personality disorder (OCPD). 22 patients (52.4%) met the criteria for OCPD.

2. Bourne, L. & Yaroush, R. (2003, February). Stress and cognition: A cognitive psychological perspective, National Aeronautics and Space Administration, Grant Number NAG2-1561.

Stressors have been classified into two categories, "systemic" stressors and "neurogenic" or "processive" stressors. Systemic stressors include many situations that produce direct physiological threats to organisms, such as microbial infections, temperature extremes, dehydration, injuries, and malnourishment. Neurogenic/ processive stressors arise from situations that do not immediately threaten an organism's physiological homeostasis but are perceived as a potential threat, including psychological and psychosocial situations requiring significant cognitive processing for their interpretation. Traumatic-life events such as bereavement are familiar examples, but less traumatic events, such as psychosocial pressures from interpersonal relationships and work place settings, are also effective activators of physiological stress.

3. Echolalia commonly refers to language learning, language development, and communication in autism. It is the immediate or delayed echoing or repetition of whole, unanalyzed expressions or reciprocation. The purpose of echolalia is unclear, but it has been believed to serve a number of functions, including conversation maintenance, communication, self-soothing and verbal rehearsal.

From the 2012 edition, DSM-IV-TR, used by professionals in a wide array of contexts, including psychiatrists and other physicians, psychologists, social workers, nurses, occupational and rehabilitation therapists, and counselors, Echolalia in the Autism Spectrum Disorder: Stereotyped or repetitive speech, motor movements, or use of objects

4. Lists of Triggers, compiled from websites, interviews, and personal correspondences.

Auditory Triggers: Sounds Associated with Eating
- chewing sounds

- crunchy sounds
- eating sounds
- gum popping
- gum smacking
- hard candy being bounced around in a mouth
- lip smacking
- slurping

## Auditory Triggers: Non-Eating/chewing Sounds Made by the Mouth or Throat

- "ahhhhs" sound after drinking
- breathing through the mouth
- burping
- clearing of throat
- coughing
- flossing
- gravelly voices
- gulping
- coughing up phlegm
- hiccups
- humming
- nail biting
- nasally voices (especially female)
- repetitive throat clearing
- "S" sound
- silverware hitting or scraping teeth
- snoring
- soft breathing
- spitting
- swallowing
- teeth sucking
- throat clearing
- wet mouth sounds
- wheezing
- whistling
- yawning

## Auditory Triggers: Sounds Made by the Nose

- nose whistling
- sniffing
- breathing through the nose

## Auditory Triggers: Sounds Made by the Human Body

- kissing (in movies)
- knuckle / joint popping
- laugh tracks (on tv)
- muffled talking
- overused word
- rubbing hands together or feet together

- singing
- soft speaking/whispering
- talking with mouth open

## Auditory Triggers: Repetitive Sounds Made by People
- clicking pens
- clicking computer mouse
- clicking remote control
- cracking open pistachios
- dishes hitting together/washing dishes
- feet shuffling/footsteps
- flip flops on floor
- food wrappers rustling
- high heels on floor
- jingling coins or keys in a pocket
- nail clipping
- nails tapping
- newspaper or magazine turning
- paper or plastic bags rustling
- pencil tapping
- repetition of words or sounds
- snapping fingers
- tapping
- texting on a phone
- typing on a key board
- writing on paper with nothing between the paper and the desk

## Auditory Triggers: Repetitive Sounds, Other
- clock ticking
- hangers clicking together-- like in clothing store
- rubbing noises
- scratching
- silverware on dishes
- squeezing of water bottles
- tape or paper tearing
- tires on wet pavement
- tools hitting a hard surface
- walking sticks – Metal
- water dripping

## Auditory Triggers: Machine-Made Sounds
- beeping
- dentist drill
- droning sounds
- tv (in the background)
- sound indicators in the car
- security systems
- squeaky windshield wipers

Auditory Triggers: Animal Sounds
- bird sounds
- crickets
- dogs barking
- dogs/cats licking
- dogs drinking
- doves cooing
- frogs

Visual Triggers: face/mouth
- seeing someone chew gum (no sound)
- seeing someone eat (no sound)
- hands near mouth
- nail biting (no sound)

Visual Triggers: hand/motion
- hair twirling/ hand touching Hair
- stroking/pulling moustache or beard
- pointing

Visual Triggers: repetitive body motion
- fidgeting/thumb twiddling
- legs swinging
- legs shaking
- repetitive rocking
- swinging motions

Olfactory
- strong body odor—perspiration
- strong body odor—perfume

Personal Space/Contact
- someone tapping or kicking your chair
- someone sitting next to you draping their arm on the back of your chair
- someone standing behind you on a line is too close
- movement out of the corner of one's eye

CHAPTER 5: What's the Diagnosis

1. From DSM-IV-TR Criteria for Posttraumatic Stress Disorder. American Psychiatric Association. (2000). *Diagnostic and statistical manual of mental disorders* (Revised 4th ed.). Washington, DC. (The DSM has been updated at the time of this printing. It is the DSM-V edition.)

The manual defines a mental disorder as "a clinically significant behavioral or psychological syndrome or pattern that occurs in an individual and that is associated with present distress (a painful symptom) or disability (impairment in one or more important areas of functioning) or with a significantly increased risk of suffering death, pain or disability. In addition, this syndrome or pattern must not be merely an expectable and culturally sanctioned response to a particular event, e.g. the death of a loved one.

Whatever its original cause, it must currently be considered a manifestation of a behavioral, psychological or biological dysfunction in the individual. Neither deviant behavior, e.g., political, religious, or sexual, nor conflicts that are primarily between the individual and society are mental disorders unless the deviance or conflict is a symptom of a dysfunction in the individual, as described above."

APA Diagnostic Classification DSM-IV-TR, list of disorders
- Adjustment Disorders
- Anxiety Disorders
- Delirium, Dementia, and Amnestic and Other Cognitive Disorders
- Disorders Usually First Diagnosed in Infancy, Childhood, or Adolescence
- Dissociative Disorders
- Eating Disorders
- Factitious Disorders
- Impulse-Control Disorders
- Mental Disorders Due to a General Medical Condition
- Mood Disorders
- Other Conditions That May Be a Focus of Clinical Attention
- Personality Disorders
- Schizophrenia and Other Psychotic Disorders
- Sexual and Gender Identity Disorders
- Sleep Disorders
- Somatoform Disorders
- Substance-Related Disorders

2. Anxiety coded for insurance purposes as Medical code: 2012 ICD-9-CM Diagnosis Code 300.00: Anxiety state, unspecified
- Feeling of distress or apprehension whose source is unknown.
- Unpleasant, but not necessarily pathological, emotional state resulting from an unfounded or irrational perception of danger; compare with fear and clinical anxiety.

- Vague uneasy feeling of discomfort or dread accompanied by an autonomic response (the source often nonspecific or unknown to the individual); a feeling of apprehension caused by anticipation of danger. It is an alerting signal that warns of impending danger and enables the individual to take measures to deal with threat.
- Apprehension or fear of impending actual or imagined danger, vulnerability, or uncertainty.
- Apprehension of danger and dread accompanied by restlessness, tension, tachycardia, and dyspnea unattached to a clearly identifiable stimulus.
- Term was discontinued in 1997. In 2000, the term was removed from all records containing it, and replaced with *Anxiety Disorders*, its postable counterpart.
- Short description: Anxiety state NOS [not otherwise specified].

3. Retrieved online from:
http://www.thesun.co.uk/sol/homepage/woman/health/health/3539291/Woman-sufferes-from-a-phobia-to-the-sound-of-people-eating.html#ixzz2CtJ9WZMh

Alison Smith-Squire, Eat Quietly or Mum will Lose her Lunch, 21st April 2011.

*MUM Cheryl Houghton has a bizarre phobia – she can't bear the sound of other people EATING. Cheryl, 30, has to listen to an iPod to drown the sound of husband Jeff munching his dinner. She said: "Many people don't take me seriously when I say I can't stand hearing others eat or drink but it ruins my life. "Just the sound of someone gulping down a glass of water is enough to bring me out in a cold sweat. "If I'm shopping and hear someone munching crisps, I have to leave the shop. Going to the cinema is out of the question. "Even the thought of sitting there surrounded by people eating popcorn terrifies me." Going on holiday is an issue too: "On a plane I have to wear earphones otherwise a person sitting next to me with a glass of wine can put me into a state of terrible anxiety."*

*Cheryl, from Helston, Cornwall, believes her phobia began at the age of 13. She said: "I was watching a chat show when someone on it mentioned she hated hearing people noisily crunching apples.*

*"That evening at teatime it was as if someone had switched on supersonic hearing. From then on it was as if every sound people made when they ate or drank was magnified."*

*She said: "I always tried to cover up my condition and feel it's my fault so I would never say anything to anyone.
"However, if I saw someone opening a packet of biscuits, I would make an excuse and go to the loo or put the kettle on. Two years ago Cheryl tried hypnosis to cure her phobia. She said: "I was barely out of the consultation room when I heard someone crunching and felt ill. It hadn't worked."*

4. For full diagnostic criteria, see DSM-IV-TR Criteria for Posttraumatic Stress Disorder. American Psychiatric Association. (2000). *Diagnostic and statistical manual of mental disorders* (Revised 4th ed.). Washington, DC

5. DSM-IV-TR Criteria for Posttraumatic Stress Disorder. American Psychiatric Association. (2000). *Diagnostic and statistical manual of mental disorders* (Revised 4th ed.). Washington, DC:

1.  The person has been exposed to a traumatic event in which both of the following were present:
    (1) The person experienced, witnessed, or was confronted with an event or events that involved actual or threatened death or serious injury, or a threat to the physical integrity of self or others.
    (2) The person's response involved intense fear, helplessness, or horror. Note: In children, this may be expressed instead by disorganized or agitated behavior.
2.  The traumatic event is persistently re-experienced in one (or more) of the following ways:
    (3) Recurrent and intrusive distressing recollections of the event, including images, thoughts, or perceptions. Note: In young children, repetitive play may occur in which themes or aspects of the trauma are expressed.
    (4) Recurrent distressing dreams of the event. Note: In children, there may be frightening dreams without recognizable content.

(5) Acting or feeling as if the traumatic event were recurring (includes a sense of reliving the experience; illusions, hallucinations, and dissociative flashback episodes, including those that occur on awakening or when intoxicated). Note: In young children, trauma-specific reenactment may occur.

(6) Intense psychological distress at exposure to internal or external cues that symbolize or resemble an aspect of the traumatic event.

(7) Physiological reactivity on exposure to internal or external cues that symbolize or resemble an aspect of the traumatic event.

3. Persistent avoidance of stimuli associated with the trauma and numbing of general responsiveness (not present before the trauma), as indicated by three (or more) of the following:

(8) Efforts to avoid thoughts, feelings, or conversations associated with the trauma

(9) Efforts to avoid activities, places, or people that arouse recollections of the trauma

(10) Inability to recall an important aspect of the trauma

(11) Markedly diminished interest or participation in significant activities

(12) Feeling of detachment or estrangement from others

(13) Restricted range of affect (e.g., unable to have loving feelings)

(14) Sense of a foreshortened future (e.g., does not expect to have a career, marriage, children, or a normal lifespan)

4. Persistent symptoms of increased arousal (not present before the trauma), as indicated by two (or more) of the following:

(1) Difficulty falling or staying asleep

(2) Irritability or outbursts of anger

(3) Difficulty concentrating

(4) Hypervigilance

(5) Exaggerated startle response

5. Duration of the disturbance (symptoms in Criteria B, C, and D) is more than 1 month.

6. The disturbance causes clinically significant distress or impairment in social, occupational, or other important areas of functioning.

*Specify if:* Acute: if duration of symptoms is less than 3 months
Chronic: if duration of symptoms is 3 months or more
*Specify if:* With Delayed Onset: if onset of symptoms is at least 6 months after the stressor.

6. Retrieved online from:
http://drphil.com/slideshows/slideshow/5518/?id=5518&slide=1&showID=1374& review=&versionID=.

> *"I am annoyed by sniffing, people clearing their throats, coughing," Andrea says. "I wear my earplugs every single place I go. Aside from the sniffing, there are a lot of other things that*
> *annoy me. One of the biggest things is we have this dog in our neighborhood. When she barks, it drives me nuts," she says. "Dry chomping – it's a term I made up. It's like chomping with no food in your mouth. I don't even know how to explain it. It's like this slobbering noise. It's disgusting... So, Dr. Phil, am I the only one who's annoyed by this stuff?" Andrea tells Dr. Phil the noises that annoy her are like fingernails on a chalkboard for a normal person. "It's, like, 10 times worse," she says. Andrea guesses that it has something to do with anxiety.*

> *"I want to answer this very seriously for you because I know it's really bothering you," Dr. Phil says. "The first thing you have to do is rule out any kind of medical causation here. You should talk to someone, because some people can have hypersensitive hearing, so it's like a radio turned up all the way, all the time, and there are things that can be done to desensitize you in that regard, if that's what's going on."... Dr. Phil explains that she can get control of this anxiety in as little as 10 to 12 hours.*

7. Sensory problems become a disorder when the impact is chronic and/or disrupts everyday life. There are many ways in which a SPD can present. The following list is not exhaustive:

- Heightened reactivity to sound, touch or movement
- Under-reactivity to certain sensations e.g. not noticing name being called, being touched, high pain threshold
- Seeking increased amounts of auditory, tactile or movement input e.g. making noises to self, constantly touching objects/people, being "on the go"
- Appears lethargic/disinterested; appearing to mostly be in own world

- Difficulty regulating own behavioural and emotional responses; increased tantrums, emotional reactive, need for control, impulsive behaviours, easily frustrated or overly compliant
- Easily distracted, poor attention and concentration
- Poor motor skills; appears clumsy, reduced coordination, balance and motor planning skills, poor handwriting skills
- Difficulty mastering activities of daily living e.g. dressing, tying shoe laces, self-feeding
- Poor sleep patterns
- Restricted eating habits or picky eater
- Difficulty engaging in grooming tasks e.g. hair-brushing, hair-washing, nail cutting etc
- Loves movement and appears to have a need for intense pressure, continually seeking this out e.g. constant spinning, running around, jumping, crashing in objects/people
- Avoids movement based equipment e.g. swings, slides etc
- Appears floppy or has 'low muscle tone', tires easily and is often slumped in postures
- Does things with too much force, has big movements, moves fast, writes too light or too hard
- Delayed communication and social skills, hard to engage in two-way interactions
- Prefers to play on their own or difficulty in knowing how to play with other children
- Difficulty accepting changes in routine or transitioning between tasks
- Difficulty engaging with peers and sustaining friendships

8. Schröder A, Vulink, N., & Denys, D. (2013). Misophonia: diagnostic criteria for a new psychiatric disorder. PLoS One.; 8(1). Retrieved online from: http://www.ncbi.nlm.nih.gov/pubmed/23372758

The symptom pattern of misophonia shares a number of features with other DSM-IV-TR and ICD-10 diagnoses: specific phobia, post-traumatic stress disorder (PTSD), social phobia, obsessive compulsive disorder (OCD), intermittent explosive disorder, emotionally unstable personality disorder, borderline personality disorder, antisocial personality disorder, OCPD, and autism spectrum disorders (ASD), and sensory processing disorders (SPD) and phonophobia. None of the diagnostic categories fit the whole symptom pattern of misophonia.

CHAPTER 7: The Trigger Brain

1. Gruters, K. and Groh, J. (2012). Sounds and beyond: multisensory and other non-auditory signals in the inferior colliculus. *Frontiers in Neural Circuits*, 6, 96.

The IC gets input from several auditory areas in the brain stem, and sends input to the auditory portion of the thalamus. Cells within it are sensitive not only to auditory signals, but to visual and somatosensory information as well. There are cells that are capable of responding directly to visual stimuli without an accompanying sound. There are cells whose auditory responses are modulated by a concurrent visual stimulus.

Non-auditory signals may contribute to distinguishing self-generated sounds from external sounds. They contribute to accurately perceiving communication sounds which are useful in suppressing self-generated noise, including vocalizations like throat clearing, chewing sounds (mastication), and breathing sounds (respiration). The output of the IC may serve to inform the thalamus and cortex when throat clearing, chewing, and heavy breathing comes from the self as opposed to others.

2. Saalmann, Y., Pinsk, M., Wang, L., Li, X & Kastner, S. (2012, August). The pulvinar regulates information transmission between cortical areas based on attention demands. Science, 337(6095), 753-756.

Studies of pulvinar neurons' response to visual stimuli have demonstrated increased activation if the stimulus has behavioral relevance. The pulvinar neurons respond more vigorously to 'behaviorally relevant' targets than to unattended stimuli.

3. To examine amygdala responses to aversive auditory stimuli, healthy human subjects were exposed to unpleasant sounds while regional cerebral blood flow (rCBF) was assayed. Eight subjects, all of whom described themselves as reactive to aversive sounds, participated in the study. Relative to white noise, the aversive sounds produced significant rCBF increases in the lateral amygdala region. Significant activations also localized to other brain regions, including the insula, right auditory association cortices, putamen, and thalamus.

4. Moayedi, M. & Weissman-Fogel, I. (2009). Is the insula the "how much" intensity coder? *Journal of Neurophysiology*, 102, 1345-1347.

The anterior insula projects to the amygdala; the ventral anterior projects mostly to the limbic system. In turn, it receives a direct projection from the [basal part of the ventral medial nucleus of the] thalamus and a large input from the central nucleus of the amygdala. In a 2009 study, areas believed to encode sensory stimulus magnitude in the brain may, in fact, be coding salience and appropriately reorienting attention.

5. Cauda, F., D'Agataa, F., Saccoa, K., Ducaa, S., Geminiania, G. & Vercellid, A. (2011, March). Functional connectivity of the insula in the resting brain. *Neuroimage*, 55(1), 8-23. Retrieved online from: http://www.academia.edu/1105776/Functional_connectivity_of_the_insula _in_the_resting_brain.
It is suspected that altered patterns of connectivity between the anterior and posterior locations of the insula rfmay underlie or predispose individuals to neuropsychiatric diseases.


CHAPTER 8: Brain Circuitry and Triggers

1. Many theoretical models of connectivity in the human brain are not actually based on studies of the human brain. Many representations of circuitry are from other animals, such as cats, rats, and monkeys. Yet conscious analytic thought, recollection of memories, and the indisputable striving to understand the world uniquely belong to the human mind.

2. Adolphs, R. (2002, April). Neural systems for recognizing emotion. *Current Opinion in Neurobiology*, 12(2), 169-77.

Multi-sensory information from the cortex modulates the amygdala's emotionally-based response of flight. This argument stems from the theory that the amygdala calls upon information from higher thinking centers of the brain (cognitive resources) to help resolve ambiguity in the environment.

3. In specific, the CE connects with the central grey, the lateral and paraventricular hypothalamus.

4. Both valence and salience are important terms in the study of a stimulus. Valence refers to the value of a stimulus, either positive (pleasant) or negative (unpleasant). Salience is a term used in the study of perception and cognition that refers to any aspect of a stimulus that stands out. Salience may be the result of emotional, motivational or cognitive factors. Salience is thought to determine attentional selection. Retrieved online from: http://en.wikipedia.org/wiki/Salience_%28neuroscience%29.

5. Projections from sensory association cortices, such as the auditory cortex, have many interconnections with cortical regions of the brain, with each region having both generalized and specialized functions. As stimuli are processed, refined, and mingled with cognitive thought, their neural representations are taken via pathways back to the sub-cortical brain centers responsible for fleeing and responses.

6. Activity in the auditory cortex and the amygdala show a high degree of functional connectivity, and it is only recently that scientists have started to investigate what the cortex to sub-cortex pathways do. The auditory cortex provides feedback to "lower" parts of the brain, and part of that feedback is the modulation of acoustic features. Electrical stimulation of small portions of the auditory cortex has been shown to alter the frequency tuning and other response properties of the midbrain. These findings suggest a critical selective filtering role that enables us to pay particular attention to certain aspects of our auditory environment while ignoring others.

7. The OFC integrates sensory and somatovisceral information and establishes an initial value-based representation of an object. The representation includes external sensory features of the object, along with its impact on the stable resting-state of the body.

8. Allen, G., Saper, C., Hurley, K & Cechetto, D. (1991, September). Organization of visceral and limbic connections in the insular cortex of the rat. *Journal of Comparative Neurology*, 311(1), 1–16.

The lateral hypothalamic area and the amygdala are diffusely distributed over the different regions of the insular cortex. This organization may support a role for the insular cortex in the integration of autonomic responses with ongoing behavior and emotion.

9. Suvak, M., & Feldman- Barrett, L. (2011, February). Considering PTSD from the perspective of brain processes: a psychological construction approach. *Trauma Stress*, 24(1), 3–24.

The cortex exerts a nuanced and complex influence over autonomic nuclei in the brainstem and even in the spinal cord. Some of the direct connections from cortical regions to autonomic centers in the brainstem are excitatory and enhance autonomic reactivity. Other connections from cortical regions have an inhibitory effect on the autonomic regions, putting the brake on autonomic reactivity. It is possible that at times, cortical regions are enhancing autonomic reactivity because part of their inhibitory action might be selectively impaired.

10. Pessoa, L. & Adolphs, R. (2010, November) Emotion processing and the amygdala: from a 'low road' to 'many roads' of evaluating biological significance. *Nature Reviews Neuroscience*, 11(11), 773–783.

It has been proposed that the pulvinar is involved in attention, visual awareness, and/or distracter-filtering, consistent with data from neuroimaging and lesion studies in humans. Pulvinar neurons increase firing in response to visual stimuli if attention is paid to the stimulus or if the stimulus has behavioral relevance.

11. Pessoa, L. & Adolphs, R. (2010, November) Emotion processing and the amygdala: from a 'low road' to 'many roads' of evaluating biological significance. *Nature Reviews Neuroscience*, 11(11), 773–783.

If the brain associates visual phenomenon with auditory phenomenon, such as the sight of someone chewing, then one would predict that the response to those visual stimuli should be fast. There is evidence that visual processing from the cortex is as fast as subcortical processing. Electrophysiological responses evoked by visual stimuli can be modulated by the emotional content of the stimuli, and this modulation has been reported to occur at short latencies. In some studies in humans, responses occur within 100 ms of stimulus onset. Short-latency (100–150 ms) electrophysiological responses in the OFC have been associated with discrimination of the valence of a visual stimulus.

## CHAPTER 9: The Brain and Multi-Sensory Processing

1. Schroeder, C. & Foxe, J. (2005). Multisensory contributions to low-level 'unisensory' processing. *Current Opinion in Neurobiology*, 15, 454–458.

The auditory cortex, which assesses, evaluates, and stores auditory stimuli and memory, is influenced by visual input and somatosensory (arising from skin and internal organs) input. The auditory cortex, with the overlap of other senses such as vision and internal body state, gives enhanced processing of the evaluation of a sound. The perceptual experience of something heard is associated with other sensory modalities. In this way, a particular sound becomes more than just a sound. It becomes a small story, richer in detail, providing additional information that within seconds can be fed to the higher centers of the brain that call for decision-making.

CHAPTER 10: A Developmental Disorder: What Can Sudden Onset Tell Us?

1. Filley, C. (Jan 1, 2005) Why the White Brain Matters, The Dana Foundation. Retrieved online from: http://www.dana.org/news/cerebrum/detail.aspx?id=832

Although the precise reason for pruning is unknown, it is speculated that the brain is developing on the basis of experience and pruning rids the system of unneeded connections. Due to the brain's plasticity, these connections are continuously remodeled throughout life.

2. The brain continues to increase in total volume from birth until approximately 14 years of age. Total white matter volume continues to increase into the early 20s. The grey matter in the occipital and temporal lobes continues to increase until 20 years of age.

3. Toga, A., Thompson, P., & Sowell, E. (2006, March). Mapping brain maturation. *Trends in Neuroscience*, 29(3), 148–159.

Data from childhood-onset schizophrenia patients vs. healthy controls were analyzed using brain-mapping methods developed to detect subtle changes in the cortex. Healthy subjects lost gray matter at a subtle rate of 1% to 2% per year in the parietal cortices, with very little detectable change in the other lobes of the brain. By contrast, the childhood-onset schizophrenia patients showed a rapid progressive loss of gray matter in superior frontal and temporal cortices, reaching 3% to 4% per year in some regions.

4. While different brain abnormalities have been observed for different disorders, most of the abnormalities observed in the quantitative MRI studies of children with developmental disorders have been relatively subtle. Statistical differences can be found when comparing groups of children with a particular disorder vs. non-affected controls, but cannot be found within any one individual.

5. Kostović, I., Judaš, M., & Sedmak, G. (2011, May). Developmental history of the subplate zone, subplate neurons and interstitial white matter neurons: relevance for schizophrenia. *International Journal of Developmental Neuroscience, 29*(3), 193-205.

There is speculation that cortical cells called GABAergic interneurons act as "gates" at the interface where neurons of emotional center pathways and those of modulatory afferent pathways enter the prefrontal cortex. An enlarged population of the GABA interneurons may inhibit limbic and modulatory inputs.

This leads to a functional disconnectivity between the prefrontal and limbic cortex in the adolescent brain. In other words, the part of the adolescent brain that has a strong influence on emotions is disconnected from the part of the brain that modulates and controls decision making. Since the prefrontal cortex is involved in decision making and impulse control, the emotional center has greater free reign to act. This leads to impulsive behavior, as thoughts and actions are removed from conscious deliberation.

6. Milham, M., Nugent, A., Drevets, W., Dickstein, D., Leibenluft, E., Ernst , M., Charney, D. Pine, D. (2005). Selective reduction in amygdala volume in pediatric anxiety disorders: a voxel-based morphometry investigation. *Biological Psychiatry*, 57(9), 961–966.

A comparison of children and adolescents with generalized anxiety disorder had larger right and total amygdala volume as compared to age-matched healthy controls. An analysis of children with an average age of 12.9 years who had separation anxiety, social phobia, or generalized anxiety disorder (GAD) reported a significant grey matter volume reduction within the left amygdala of children when compared to healthy controls.

7. do Rosario-Campos, M., Leckman, J., Mercadante, M., Shavitt, R., da Silva Prado, H., Sada, P., Zamignani, D., & Miguel, E. (2001). Adults with early-onset obsessive-compulsive disorder. *American Journal of Psychiatry*, 158, 1899-1903.

Obsessive-compulsive disorder (OCD) is a neuropsychiatric disorder that has two discrete onsets, with age 10 often used as a mean threshold for early onset, and age 17 for late-onset. Early onset is associated with higher scores on the Yale-Brown Obsessive Compulsive Scale and higher frequencies of tic-like compulsions. To date, little is known about the cause of early OCD onset although genetic factors are suspected.

CHAPTER 11: Emotions Overview

1. Overt aggression is typically associated with anger; implicit is the assumption that the two are closely connected neurologically. There exists

the possibility that circuits that stimulate fear and aggression might be separate from circuits of anger; fear and aggression might not be stimulated by "Sound-Rage," whereas the circuits that produce anger are stimulated in "Sound-Rage." If this is the case, then the "Sound-Rage" disorder provides fertile ground for the further study of aggression as well as provides new direction for the study on anger.

## CHAPTER 13: Anger and Disgust

1. Disgust is typically associated with things that are regarded as unclean or infectious, and is considered by many theorists to be one of the basic emotions along with anger, happiness, and fear. Disgust is characterized by a feeling of revulsion or profound disapproval aroused by exposure to something unpleasant or offensive and often manifests as nausea or particular facial expressions. In the logic of evolution, disgust is survival by aversion, a primal, strong, and automatic response.

## CHAPTER 14: Hypervigilance and Attention to Danger

1. Surguladze, S. Brammer, M.J., Young, A.W., Andrew, C., Travis, M.J., Williams, S.C. &Phillips, M.L. (2003). A preferential increase in the extrastriate response to signals of danger. *NeuroImage*. 19, 1317–1328.

The fusiform gyrus, a cortical area that responds to faces, is activated more strongly by fearful facial expressions compared to other emotions.

## CHAPTER 15: Cognition: How the Brain Thinks about Triggers

1. Neural systems for recognizing emotion, Adolphs, R. (2002). Current Opinion in Neurobiology, Elsevier Science Ltd.

One argument is that the amygdala triggers cognitive resources— information from higher thinking centers of the brain—to help resolve ambiguity in the environment. The amygdala is where trigger-stimuli ramp up the body into a physiological state of fleeing and where emotional memories become fixed. Initially, the amygdala receives information before there is cortical reasoning. Thus, the memory that is fixed in the amygdala represents features and fragments that do not necessarily coincide with perceptions occurring in the cortex. This creates a basic conundrum for the thinking, evaluative mind.

Made in the USA
Middletown, DE
02 December 2017